Crevice

A Life Between Worlds

By

Anna Redsand

Winner of the
Kenneth Johnston
Nonfiction Book Contest
2024

Semifinalist in the
River Teeth Literary Nonfiction
Book Prize Contest for 2024

Choeofpleirn Press

ISBN:
(print) 979-8-9911790-8-9
(digital) 979-8-9911790-9-6

Crevice ii

I would call Anna Redsand's book "White Rez Kid" because that's what it's about—not just the White kid who grew up on the Rez, but how the Rez is part of her life now—how her unique perspective has risen from the crevice that lies between cultures. Diné and Bilagáana people both need to hear Anna's voice.

~Gloria J. Emerson (Diné), *At the Hems of the Lowest Clouds: Meditations on Navajo Landscapes*

In *Crevice: A Life Between Worlds*, Anna blends a deeply personal memoir with a wisdom and grace that resonates beyond the particulars of her own story. I was in tears by the end of the first page, in an exhale of relief and recognition. This book offers a clear-eyed gaze on the deeply complex experience of growing up in a 'home not home'. Beautifully blending memories and searing self-inquiry, Anna offers important insights into the ways in which the politics of colonialization, and spiritual exceptionalism infiltrate the daily lived experience of so many Third Culture Kids. I especially appreciated her sensitive observations around language, the grief and loss that so many experience when caught in the 'mine not mine' whirlpool of power dynamics surrounding this most basic vehicle of human connectedness. Anna uses her story to offer gentle accompaniment to all those who will recognize their own stories in her own, but she goes beyond this to invite us to consider the best question of all, 'now what?' In sharing her own processes around navigating restorative belonging as 'A Good Stranger', she offers the best kind of guidance to those of us seeking to find our own way – the guidance of one who has walked before us.

~Rachel Cason, *Incredible Lives and the Courage to Live Them: Thoughts of a Third Culture Kid Therapist*

Crevice is a tender excavation of a life lived between cultures, not only from the perspective of a white woman raised by Calvinist missionaries on the Navajo Reservation, but of a lesbian growing up in straight culture. Ever the seeker, the content of Redsand's essays is rare, the perspective even rarer, and the hard-won insights she arrives at are all the more valuable for it.

~Gabriel Kruis, *Acid Virga*

Crevice iv

To my longtime friends and colleagues

Louise Benally
Gloria Emerson
Rose Fasthorse Nofchissey
Ed Singer

and

to the hope that
diversity, equity, and inclusion
will become a worldwide reality

Contents

"We are made of stories, and if we don't know them—the ones that make us—how can we ever be fully realized? How can we ever be who we really are?"

~Morgan Talty (Penobscot), *Fire Exit*

Author's Note:
Language Matters

Language matters. It especially matters when we talk about contact among cultures and the interstices between them. It matters whether I choose to write *reservation* or *Navajo Nation* or *Dinétah*. These three expressions delineate the same locale, yet each *means* something different, and the difference is significant. The language we use to talk about the legacy of colonization––a legacy that virtually no one on Earth escapes––is important. This inheritance carries particular weight in these thirteen essays. Accordingly, I have privileged certain words over others, hoping to bring about a small measure of healing by contributing, to a miniscule degree, to the monumental task of decolonization. Thus:

- Diné (Navajos' name for themselves) over Navajo;
- Diné bizaad over Diné language or Navajo language or simply Navajo;
- Dinétah, Navajo Country, Navajo Nation, the Nation over reservation;
- Indigenous or Native over Indian or Native American;
- Bilagáana (the Diné name for Whites) in addition to White;

• When *Black*, *White*, or *Brown* refer to individuals or a group identified by one of these colors, the words are capitalized as proper nouns.
• Words in Diné bizaad are not italicized, except for emphasis or when referred to as words themselves; this is in a recognition of their legitimacy equal to the legitimacy of English.

Introduction

Crevice is a memoir in thirteen related, stand-alone essays, seven of which have been previously published. The stories and reflections tell about the life of a White girl, and later an adult, living within the fissure that lies between Diné and Bilagáana cultures. In that place, I belonged and didn't belong; it was Home Not Home. The story is about what I saw from within the cleft that existed between the two worlds, which was often different from what either Diné or Bilagáanas saw from either side of that space. It is about what that was like in the fifties and sixties when I was a child and life was simply that—life. My life. It is about what I am left with now in the twenty-first century—both richness and poverty. It is about grappling with my settler heritage, the riches I was given in my time in Dinétah, and about the obligations that perhaps come with those experiences. It is about what I have created and hope still to create from both of my inheritances. Each essay reflects in some way on the identity that evolves when someone spends a lifetime between distinctly different cultures. The far-reaching effects of colonization and occupation that continue today in *Dinétah* are an unavoidable part of the landscape and necessarily play a significant role in my observations and thoughts.

Part I, Ground, contains four essays that recreate early days in the author's life, moving in each case from childhood into adulthood. "Fissures and Crenellations," the first piece, situates the reader in Dinétah and shows for the first time the land of In Between. "In and Out" is about the exigencies of boarding school life as lived by a White girl, as viewed by me, and as told to me by my Diné friends. "Some Things Were True" is about both Diné and Bilagáana beliefs and practices regarding death—about what was real in both cultures and what perhaps was not, about sameness and difference. "In the Girls' Room" shows how, throughout my life, I have parsed what others and I observed of my parents' contrasting ways as guests in Dinétah. It tells how I have attempted to make sense of what I heard and saw and to find my own path in that land.

Part II, Self, contains five essays and has a particular focus on the search for identity. "Border Town," a hybrid essay, shows the everyday devastation that exists in and because of towns that border the Navajo Nation. It tells of the nature of borders, about how I tried to find my place in Gallup, New Mexico, a town on the edge of the Nation—the town that in many ways describes who I am. Four further essays address questions of identity that have persisted into my adulthood. "Naturalization" is about how an interracial partnership of seven years left an imprint on my interactions with my Black college students. "A Good Stranger" is a braided essay that explores a search for spiritual identity within the milieu of three distinct cultural identities. "Tongues" is an experimental essay, exploring human and animal existence through the multiple meanings in multiple languages—denotative, connotative, and idiomatic—of the word "tongue." In "The Importance of Clear" I discover through the lens of language that I may possess a lasting identity of my own.

Part III, Passage, offers the final four essays and moves the writer and hence the reader toward resolution. "Racial Injustice Benefited Me" is a flash essay that details a very small number of ways in which systemic racism benefited me as a child living in the Navajo Nation. In "Being Third" I examine Other as a possible identity, following a path away from binary thinking. "The Obligation" examines the idea that those who have inhabited the cracks and crevices of society may be uniquely equipped to bridge our many cultural gaps—that in fact, we may have a duty to do so. "A Reckoning," the final essay in the collection, represents a coming to terms with just what is my place in the worlds I have inhabited and a recognition of who I am within the fissure between them.

Names have been changed, except for family members and public figures, to protect individual privacy.

PART I
GROUND

Crevice 2

Fissures and Crenellations

"How do the stories we tell about ourselves
in relationship to place
shape our perceptions of place?"
~Terry Tempest Williams, *Red*

We drove across endless white alkaline flats into the Navajo Nation. It was the first time. No trees, just a few gray saltbushes, some sage, shocks of platinum grasses. We drove over dried-up washes that looked like long, narrow jigsaw puzzles. Across the plains to our left ran the blue-black Chuska Range, the off-center spine of the Nation. Far away on the right, tiny rust, orange, and purple boxes lined the horizon; I would learn to call them *mesas*. Overhead, all around us, wherever land met sky and into the distance above, rose the brilliant, inverted blue bowl. It was 1952. I was four years old.

We rode in the big green Chevrolet Carryall, a forerunner to today's Suburban. My father drove, and my mother sat in the back seat with me and my younger brother and baby sister. We were on our way to what my parents called *God's Work*. Missionary work. I would be proud of their work until I began to understand how it was an integral part of the devastation that is colonization; then I would take on a task that could return some measure of what proselytizing had taken away.

Somewhere between Naschitti—the Place of the Badger—and Sheep Springs, my father stopped the car to let a flock of sheep cross the road. While we waited for them, my mother pointed to a small, domed structure made of logs and earth. "It's a hogan," she said.

"What's a hogan?"

"It's a Navajo home."

I liked how its roundness hugged the flat land, small and cozy looking. "Are we going to live in a hogan?"

"No. If you live in a hogan you have to chop wood and haul water. You have to do everything by hand—wash clothes, butcher sheep for food, herd sheep—like that lady is doing." She pointed to the woman who followed the flock we waited for—a woman wearing a long dark green satin skirt, a gray jacket, and a paisley scarf tied tight under her chin. "There wouldn't be any time left for Daddy to do God's Work," my mother added.

In an afterthought she said, "They sleep on a dirt floor on sheepskins."

The idea of sleeping on a sheepskin on the floor stirred my imagination. Wanting to live in a hogan became the first inkling of what would grow into my longing to become Other, to belong to this place and its people.

The sheep, their herder and a small yellow dog finished their trek across the road, and we started up again. As we neared the Navajo Nation town of Shiprock, the mountain range disappeared. Nothing but flatness surrounded us until, out of nowhere, the giant brown volcanic plug for which the town is named thrust its jagged peaks into the sky. I grew still in the face of something ancient, unshakeable, everlasting.

Then, "What is it?" I asked.

"Shiprock," my father said.

Crevice 4

Looking back, I understand why my young self was confused. I knew we were going to live in a place called *Shiprock*, but living within this massive rock, folded into its mysterious crenellations, seemed impossible and also frightening. I asked my father, "Are we going to live *there*?"

He laughed in the way that can humiliate a child. "No. This is the rock named *Shiprock*. We're living in the town that's named after it."

The town of Shiprock lies close to where Utah, Colorado, Arizona and New Mexico meet. On the lip of a hill, on the east end of the village, stood a two-story, square house made of gray blocks. It looked nothing like a hogan; it would be our first home in Dinétah. From then on, no matter where on Earth I find myself, I am always living on the edges of Navajo Country, just as this foreign house stood on the edge of that hill. If not physically, I will always live on those margins in the geography of my mind.

The hilltop was covered in large, smooth river rocks, left from the time when water covered vast expanses of this part of the world. The water had shrunken now to the brown flow of the San Juan River. Enormous, gnarled cottonwoods populated the banks, and willow switches waved there—gold-green in spring, scarlet in winter. Diné farmers used the water to irrigate fields and orchards.

Up there on the hill, beside the garden where my father grew corn, string beans, squash, tomatoes and peppers, I played with Bobby and Rudy Yellowhair, my first playmates in Dinétah. Most days we crouched on the ground between the garden and the garage. My father had placed peaches, cut in half, onto window screens on the garage roof so the sun could dry them. Their peachy smell came down to us while we made little Diné homesteads in the soft dirt we stole from the squash hills—hogans, sheep corrals, summer shelters, sweat lodges. This was something Diné children had been doing for years and years, centuries probably.

We didn't live long in Shiprock—a little less than a year because my father had been transferred to the mission in the small valley that was Teec Nos Pos. My mother packed our house into the pickup, and my father took several loads before we all piled in with the last one. We drove west over thirty miles of dirt road punctuated by cobbles the size of babies' heads, bumping at last down into the place that would become home. And yet, it would never really be home, though I would not understand that until I was older. Because we were not Diné, we would always be guests in Dinétah.

Where Shiprock was the gray of round river rocks, the white of the flat plains, the secretive blacks and browns of the great monolith, and the narrow strips of green edging the river, Teec Nos Pos was all color. A great rock-and-earth mound of melon pink, verdigris, mauve, violet, chocolate, peach, sorrel, gold, and cream dominated the valley. Atop the heap, gigantic sandstone blocks stood guard over us. Despite their majesty, the guardians had been given the comical name, The Three Monkeys. Dark and light greens of junipers, piñons, and scrub oak graced the valley. The indigo of the Carrizo Mountains closed off its southern end. Great cottonwoods rose above the arroyo top and gave the valley its name, *T'iis Názbas* in Diné bizaad—*A Circle of Cottonwoods*.

Teec Nos Pos became the first place where my heart set down tendrils into the Earth, and they are there still. Even now I sometimes dream of that valley. I dream that I have made a tree house in the little twisted oak that seemed so tall when I was small.

In my dream, a stream runs beneath the tree, and a huge slab of apricot-colored rock bridges the water. The bridge becomes a path that leads down to an abandoned house covered in scarlet Virginia creeper, a house that never existed, any more than my tree house did. I wander through the rooms of the white, board-and-batten house, trying to find my place. I live in this dream, looking for myself in this house. It happens again and again.

My brother Rick is two years younger than me, closest to me in age and in experience of my seven brothers. More than fifty years after we'd moved away from Teec Nos Pos, he and I took a trip there. It was the first time that just the two of us returned together. We drove the rolling highway from Shiprock and kept long silences, each in our own thoughts. Then, bringing us out of our reveries, I asked him, "How do you think of Teec Nos Pos now?"

"I think of it as the place of my Magic Years," he said without pause.

I looked over at him, a little surprised, waiting for an explanation. "There's this book about early childhood called *The Magic Years*, and at Teec, I was the age of those years." His face took on a dreamy look, reminding me of the little boy with blue-gray eyes—the boy who was always looking to someplace beyond. He said, "I remember a time when I made a circle of little stones on the dirt and sat down cross-legged in it. I was probably about five. It was by the apple tree. That tree was magical too, because of the names we gave the branches."

I smiled and nodded. We had called the branches Big and Little Buttermilk, Montana, Big and Little Texas, Wonderland. We spent hours owning the branches we sat on, negotiating trades, chattering with each other and sometimes with the traders' children or Sally and Carol Belone, the daughters of the dormitory matron up the hill.

"I was sitting in my circle," Rick went on, "trying to get a tooth loose, so I could get a nickel to go to the trading post and buy a Big Hunk candy bar. Pretty soon I was watching these lizards go in and out of crevasses in the rock ledge just above the arroyo. I could fly then, too. I had dreams that I was flying."

I asked, "Do you remember the time that Miss Mims called down because you hadn't shown up at school? I guess Mom always called if you weren't going to be there, so the principal was worried when she didn't get a call. Mom told her that she'd sent you an hour earlier. Do you remember this?"

He shook his head.

"Mom went out to look for you and found you sitting on a rock halfway up to the school, watching a pair of birds."

He laughed. "I don't remember that." In that moment, I realized something I would notice several more times on this trip. Our age and gender differences, our personalities, have given us different memories of this place.

Then he asked, "How about you? How do you think of Teec Nos Pos now?"

"I think of it as home," I said. "Even though by the time I was sixteen I knew that I was really only a visitor. I understood that I could never come back here to live. I call it Home Not Home."

It was his turn to nod. He knew the reason. Because we are Bilagáana, we can only come back to live temporarily, for professional reasons, unless we had happened to marry a Diné person.

I went on. "Still, it's more home to me than any other place on Earth. When I fill out profile questions, I say that I'm from Teec Nos Pos. I come back to Teec in my dreams." I didn't tell him the specifics of the tree-house dream, the dream of the nonexistent house where I am trying to locate myself.

Later, it came to me that the first place we think of as home is not a place. It is a memory of a place. My favorite poet, Rumi, wrote, "It is right to love your home place, but first ask, 'Where is that, really?'"

That evening Rick and I took a walk, moving through a geography of change. We strolled slowly because the boy who used to run and leap over rocks like a young goat walks with a limp now. We left the home of Rick's friend Janet, and I witnessed a change in the simple fact of Janet's house. It stands in what looks like a suburban subdivision, common now in communities all over Dinétah. Putting houses close together makes indoor plumbing and electricity easier to install, but the developments also cause some social problems, especially among young people because the traditional Diné way of living is not to live so close together. People refer to the sites as *The Housing*, no matter which community in the Nation they live in.

The Housing in Teec stands on the hilltop that rises up behind the mission, the place where we lived once. When I was a child, my summer lullabies sounded from that hill, as I lay in bed, my heavy-lidded eyes roving over The Three Monkeys. I watched the mound's colors go from gold to rose to mauve, and, at last, tones of shadowy charcoal. As stars came out, drumbeats and chanting arose from beside a hogan, the only dwelling on the hilltop in those years.

Now a large cinderblock Bureau of Indian Education (BIE) complex covers the area. There is a water tower with the name Teec Nos Pos painted on it in large black letters. There are teacherages with boarded up windows, a sprawling school with a gym and cafeteria. Everything is painted government mint-green except for the water tower, which is silver. And there is The Housing.

When Rick and I first started our ramble, walking through The Housing, we passed young Diné couples out for an evening turn, pushing baby strollers and holding the hands of toddlers. Some exchanged hellos with us. Others seemed not to see us. I felt what I often feel at times like that—as if I am a ghost. It's because the people I pass can't see me. Not really. They see the physical me, and if they think anything at all, it's probably, "old White woman." They have no way of knowing that I am rooted here, perhaps as much as they are. That I lived here before they did. That I speak some Diné bizaad. In fact, sadly, I speak more than many young Diné, perhaps more than the ones we're passing. They have no idea that The Three Monkeys formed me as much as the rocks have formed them.

In light of this, I take Terry Tempest Williams's question and twist it around so I'm asking, "How does our perception of place shape the stories we tell about ourselves?" For surely this place has shaped me, but it has created parts of me in ways that can't be seen when someone looks at me.

Rick and I ambled down the old road that was once a dirt thoroughfare for trucks laden with yellowcake uranium. Below stand tall cottonwoods that previously sheltered the former trading post. A year after we left Teec, the post burned to the ground, leaving only the trees and chunks of stone foundation, a few rotting fence posts.

My brothers and sister and I used to walk to the trading post every Saturday, each with a nickel in our pockets. On the way, we counted the green lizards that sunned themselves beside the road. Their prehistoric faces made me shiver, and I expected that one day one of them would dart at me and attack.

In those days, a broad, shaded veranda fronted the dressed sandstone store. Old men sat on a long bench, sharing news and chewing or smoking tobacco. Inside, the building was cool and dark. Wood and glass counters formed a U around the entire floor, displaying a little of every sundry imaginable—Vicks

VapoRub, Noxema face cream, Band-Aids; needles, scissors, pocketknives, and cheap eating utensils. Floor-to-ceiling shelves behind the counters held bolts of velveteen and satin, jeans and western shirts, cowboy hats shaped like oversized potato chips. Other shelves contained canned fruits and vegetables, condensed milk and sacks of Bluebird flour. From the rafters hung speckled enamel coffee pots, galvanized tubs, coils of rope, horse collars and saddles, coal scuttles, axes and shovels.

The candy counter to the immediate right of the double swinging doors was our object, and the traders, Mormon brothers, gave us plenty of time to choose among Baby Ruths, Zeroes, and penny candies. While we considered the display, I listened to the brothers speak a creole Diné that even I could hear was heavily accented and hesitant. Later I learned the name linguists gave it—*Trader Navajo*.

Outside, if women were butchering a sheep behind the hog wire fence next to the trading post, we might stand there chewing our candy, watching them lay the head and the glistening innards on the shiny inside of the sheep's skin. I listened to them talk, too, learning by osmosis the sounds that I was starting to use to form words.

Rick and I kept walking, heading toward the mission. Like everything else, it had changed. The sprawling, cobbled-together adobe we had lived in burned only a few months after we moved away. A modern frame house took its spot. The little white clapboard chapel had been replaced by a large, cinderblock affair. Two things about the mission were the same: the interpreter's modest bungalow was still there, and the oak tree stood halfway up the hill. But it had grown so small, shrunken like an old woman.

Officials said that the house and trading post fires had both been intentional, and now I wonder if the arsonist or arsonists started the fires out of resentment because the White missionaries and White traders had introduced such an alteration to a way of life that once flourished here. When I look back, that possibility seems so obvious, but when I was a child, I felt welcome, that living in Teec Nos Pos was my life, just as it was the life of everyone else who lived there.

As we came to the old places on our walk, I got out my camera several times. I needed to photograph the curve of the road from the old trading post to the mission, the rosy Three Monkeys under the pinking sky, the shaved off hilltop where I once went to school. I needed to do this to assure myself, "This is still the same place. Some things are different, and some are the same, never changing. Yes, I really did live here once. Yes, this place, really is a part of who I am."

Even more than the present-day photos, I need to look at the old ones sometimes. At home I get out a cardboard box, softening with age. In it, I find a picture of Rick and me standing in the mission yard, eating yellow slices of casaba melon from my father's garden, the Three Monkeys behind us. I'm wearing baggy shorts and a striped polo shirt, my brown hair skinned back into tight French braids. Rick, with his blond GI clip has on shorts, too, but his baby belly hangs bare over the elastic waist. The picture leaves no doubt that I was here. I am real in this place, not a ghost.

I first learned to call the immense rock formation *Shiprock*, the name Bilagáanas gave it because it resembles a clipper, a two-masted, tall-ship, rising out of the desert sea. Much later, I would learn its Diné name, *Tsé Bit'á'í, Rock with Wings*, for the lava dikes that extend outward for miles from the plug. They make the rock appear, especially from above, like a winged bird in flight. Reigning over the land as it does, it is small wonder that the rock holds a prominent place in Diné lore.

Any time we drove up and out of the valley of Teec Nos Pos for provisions or doctor visits, we passed close by the great monolith. As soon as one of us sighted it, we began to chant, "I see-e Ship-a-rock. I see-e Ship-a-rock." The rest joined in and carried on in unison until we exhausted our parents' patience. Up close, the Winged Rock resolved into mysterious vertical fissures and crenellations—feathers of the great bird. As with most features of the land called *childhood*, Shiprock was just there. When we are young, life just is; we do not know that it is perhaps remarkable. We do not know what deep impressions it is making on us. We live in the present.

A few years after Rick's and my nostalgic trip to Teec Nos Pos, I visited my friend Alice Whitegoat who lives near Shiprock. Alice is an accomplished poet and painter, my supervisor when I worked in a Native publishing house. I drove to her place, not from Teec Nos Pos, which would have put me up close to Shiprock (the rock), but from the east. I crested a rise, and off in the distance it rose—the most iconic element in the landscape of my childhood, now seldom seen. My heart leapt, its striations set to thrumming, "I am home. I am home."

Way over there, it looks small, as small as the nail on my little finger. But I know. I know the way it towers over the flats dotted with platinum grasses and a few clumps of gray-green salt weed. The rock dominates the terrain, as though nothing else can exist there—a colossal volcanic neck, its spikes piercing the brilliant blue.

"I am home. I am home." It rises from my throat as the rock itself rises from the depths of the Earth. I can't help it, as much as I try to tell myself it isn't true. "You are not home," I remonstrate. "You are here on sufferance." In childhood, there were no questions. Then I thought Dinétah belonged to me as much as it did to Rudy and Bobby Yellowhair, to Sally and Carol Belone, to the children we played with in the Teec Nos Pos arroyo, on the branches of the stunted apple tree. Now I know that wasn't how it was.

When I got to Alice's, we sat out on her patio in the dying light. I told her about how I sang when I saw the rock.

"Really?" She said. I couldn't tell what she felt.

So I added the renunciation, "I know it's not really my home. I can't claim it."

She didn't say anything. I decided her silence was tacit agreement. I said nothing more about it. I pulled back on the strings of my heart.

Our first arrival in Shiprock began a long and endless fall into the fissure that lies between two cultures. Alice sometimes shares with me her poetry in progress, and, in her songs, I hear hints of her own In Between places. Most of the Diné I know have those cracks in their lives to one degree or another because Dinétah has been under occupation for so long. Alice has expressed this crevassed life with rare eloquence and humor.

Once I wrote to her after reading one of her poems, "Even though you and I live in different In Between fissures, they could well be parallel arroyos."

Days after my visit, seeming to go back to our conversation on the patio, and apropos of nothing I had written recently, Alice wrote me. It was as though she'd been thinking about it all that time. "Shiprock. Belongs to you. Your love of Shiprock is legitimate and is for anyone, and it doesn't matter what color you are so long as your blood is red."

Whatever prompted her words, they were a blessing, and with the blessing came tears. Shiprock and Teec Nos Pos, Dinétah, are places that shape the stories I tell about myself.

In and Out

Anadarko. Chilocco. Intermountain. Riverside. Haskell. That's where the giant olive-green, formerly military buses were headed. Far away to Oklahoma, Utah, California, Kansas. I watched with admiration as teenagers hefted their shiny enameled cobalt or black footlockers into the bellies of the buses and then climbed aboard. The girls wore shirtwaist dresses with full skirts, bounced out by crinolines. The boys had on startlingly white shirts and brand new dark blue jeans, black or white cowboy hats.

   The buses lined up beside the little Bureau of Indian Affairs (BIA––now BIE) School. Each bus stood there for a whole day, while horses and wagons came and went—parents bringing their children to buses that would take them to boarding schools far away. At day's end, the buses roared off, raising dust as they passed the mission below the school—the mission where I stood watching.

   I loved the names of those places. They sounded like poetry. Anadarko—full of mystery. Chilocco—a sound of music. Intermountain—surrounded by majesty. Riverside—a green paradise. "Someday I will go to boarding school," I thought, and I knew it would be a romantic adventure.

   I was five, living on the small mission post in Teec Nos Pos in the northeast part of the Navajo Nation. My first year of school had been a kindergarten correspondence course from the Calvert

School in Baltimore. Missionaries the world over used the Calvert Course, but the next year my parents arranged with the principal that I would attend the BIA school.

"She won't be on the books," the principal said, "because it's not really legal for her to attend."

"What about report cards?"

"She'll get a report card, but we just won't include her in any of our reports to the Bureau."

My parents were sticklers for rules, so it's surprising that they agreed to this arrangement, having me be a sort of ghost student.

"We can't have her in first grade, though," Miss Mims added. "The other kids will still be learning English, and she already knows how to read." She gave my mother a look of disapproval.

On a bright September morning, my mother walked me up the hill for my first day of second grade—my first day of "real" school. The building had been constructed as a Works Project Administration (WPA) effort during the Depression and was built of native sandstone and pine vigas. We entered the cool, dark hallway, and I was assailed by unfamiliar smells that I would soon enough identify as sawdust sweeping compound, petroleum jelly, and Government commodity powdered milk, pressed pink lunchmeat, and pale yellow processed cheese.

We marched down the quiet, empty hall to my classroom. My mother knocked, and Mr. Washington answered. Silent children filled all the seats but one. Perhaps the arrangement with Miss Mims had been reached after the school year started, and that explained the already full classroom. Mr. Washington pointed to my seat, and my stomach went queasy. We started work, and between reading, coloring, adding and subtracting, I forgot that my mother was gone.

Before lunch I found out where the petroleum jelly smell came from. We girls went into a bathroom to wash up by the long porcelain trough with its many faucets.

Afterwards, the others took large dollops of Vaseline from a container in the coatroom and spread their faces, hands and arms with it to protect against the desert air. I imitated them. We trouped into the dining hall, where I learned about the powdered milk, pink meat, and pale cheese. My stomach got queasier.

Then Mrs. Belone came in, and I was happy to see her. Hers was the first familiar face I'd seen all day. She was the mother of Sally and Carol, the girls we played with in the apple tree, down in the arroyo, and in each other's houses. But she pretended that she didn't know me. "Line up! Line up! Time for your nap," she shouted.

"What?" I didn't say it out loud, but I was thinking it. "How could this be? What's happening? I don't take naps anymore. And why does Mrs. Belone sound so mean?"

She got us marching to a room with rows and rows of narrow metal beds. Striped seersucker bedspreads covered them—light and dark green ones and pink and maroon ones.

Mrs. Belone led me to a bed. "Here. You sleep here."

I tried to say, "But I don't sleep here. I don't stay here." But she was gone to some other part of the room where two boys were tussling with each other and laughing. She got that out of them right away.

I lay stiff and straight on top of my pink and maroon spread. I was terrified that this could mean I would be staying here permanently. Mrs. Belone left. My bed was near the door, and I rolled off of it, being as quiet as I could. The springs squeaked, and I stopped. No one said anything or did anything. I got to the floor, hunched over, and scooted to the door. It was open a crack, and I slipped out, looked both ways down the dark hall, saw no one, and made a dash for the outer door. It was heavy, made of metal, and it made a loud creak when I pressed the bar to open it. I squeezed through, and launched into a run. I didn't stop until I was home.

My mother looked surprised, when I dashed into the kitchen. Between gulped breaths, tears streaming, I said, "I don't want to go to school anymore. They're trying to keep me there. I had to go in this room and go to bed. They want me to stay there. And Mrs. Belone pretended like she doesn't even know me." I stopped and looked up at my mother, then I added, "And the food tastes awful."

She got on the phone to Miss Mims. I waited, hoping I wouldn't have to go back ever again, and listened to my mother's end of the conversation. When she got off the phone, I said, "Do I have to go back?"

"Yes."

"No. I don't want to. Please."

"You have to. But you can come home for lunch and have your nap here."

"But..." I was pleased but puzzled. "I don't take naps."

"We'll see about that. You have ten minutes. Then you have to go back up."

As soon as things were settled, I felt ashamed. I knew the other kids' mothers couldn't call Miss Mims and get things changed for them. I knew they had to eat the lunches, take naps in that big room, eat supper there, and sleep there at night. I was glad I didn't have to, and I felt guilty for being glad. What had happened didn't fit with my sense of fairness. But I wanted the reprieve anyway.

I became a boarding school student for the first time when I was eight. After the Teec Nos Pos BIA school, I once again took my schooling by correspondence. Halfway through fourth grade, my mother gave birth to her sixth child. My father bought our first automatic washing machine and decided I would go to Rehoboth Mission School, one hundred thirty miles away. The washing machine meant my mother no longer had to use a washboard or feed clothing and diapers through the rollers of the old wringer washer. Boarding school for me meant more time for her other chores.

I was excited. I thought I could be like those teens departing for Anadarko and Chilocco. The braids that hung to the middle of my back were cut off, leaving a severe bob to make it possible for me to take care of my own hair. My mother gave me a small tin box for my little treasures. It wasn't a footlocker like those big kids bound for Intermountain owned, but it was mine, and it was new. Everything else went into the yellow and brown suitcase my mother had used since nursing school.

Sixty-seven years after I started at Rehoboth, whenever January 24 comes around, I remember it as the anniversary of my first day of boarding school. It's not that I try to remember; I can't help it.

My father drove me to Rehoboth in the mission pickup, thirty miles over dirt and cobbles, one hundred miles over the narrow asphalt strip that was New Mexico Highway 666. He was on his way to Prescott, Arizona to be a witness in the Federal trial of someone from Teec Nos Pos. He left the pickup to be serviced by the Rehoboth maintenance crew. Over the next few days, while he was in court, that pickup became my touchstone to home. I knew on that first day that boarding school was not going to be an adventure after all, Anadarko and Riverside to the contrary.

There was a separate dorm for missionary kids, which really meant Bilagáana missionary kids. Miss Vander Weide, the white-haired matron, showed me to my basement room with its Pepto Bismol pink walls and insulated steam pipes

Crevice 20

suspended from the low ceiling. "Everyone calls me Miss Van," she said. She showed me a drawer. "Just put your suitcase on your bed for now, and you can unpack later." Mine was the narrow bed. At right angles to it was a double one. "That's where Jessie and Bonnie sleep. You'll meet them after school."

Then she walked me down the hill from the big white house that had been turned into our dorm and across the mission campus to the school. She knocked on the third and fourth grade classroom door, and a stylishly dressed, young Diné woman opened it. She and the high school Home Ec teacher were the only Diné faculty. Everyone else was Dutch American or Dutch Canadian. Neither of these women would last long at Rehoboth. Miss Silversmith brought me to the front of the room, put her arm around my shoulders and introduced me. In all my years at Rehoboth, she was the only one to give me the welcome of touch.

At noon, we lined up and marched to the Mission House where we sat ten to a table, all ages, with one adult who would ensure that we ate some of everything and cleaned our plates. After school, I went up the hill. Jessie and Bonnie were there in our room. Bonnie wore a brace on her leg, and when I saw it, I realized who she was—the missionaries' kid from Two Wells who had been bitten by a rattlesnake. She was in first grade, and I thought she seemed kind of slow. She didn't say anything at all.

Jessie was big, way bigger than me and a lot bigger than Bonnie. "I'm in sixth grade," she said. It sounded like a challenge. "What grade are you in?"

"Fourth," I squeaked.

"Ohh." The slant to her *oh* tied my stomach in knots. "Well, we had a lot more space in here before they brought your bed in." She kicked Bonnie's brace at the ankle, "Didn't we, Stupid?"

Bonnie nodded. She didn't seem to care about being kicked or being called *Stupid*.

I knew I should say something, but I didn't dare. "I'll say something next time," I thought. I already knew there would be a next time. I unpacked my suitcase and started out of the room.

"Hey! Where are you going?" Jessie asked.

I was afraid if I told her, she would follow me. I didn't say anything.

"Hey! I asked where you're going."

"Upstairs."

"Oh, are you going to tell on me? Are you a tattletale?"

I shook my head.

"What did you say?"

"I didn't ... no."

"You better not be if you know what's good for you."

Just then Wilma, who was in high school and shared the room next to ours, stepped over to our doorway. I knew her because she was the daughter of the missionary in Shiprock. "Hey, Jessie," she said. "You better leave her alone."

I said hi to Wilma and hurried toward the stairs. I knew where my father had left the pickup, and I crossed the campus, walked up behind the houses to a garage that could berth up to three vehicles. Outside the garage stood the familiar dark green pickup with the white lettering on the door: "Teec Nos Pos Christian Reformed Mission." I touched the lettering. I tried the door, but it was locked. I wanted to get in and sit on the leathery brown seat and wait for my father to come back from Prescott and take me home. Instead, I leaned in and rested my forehead against the door and felt the tears trickle down my cheeks.

I had stood there a while, when a bell gonged on the other side of campus. A thin, bent man wearing blue coveralls and rimless glasses came out of the maintenance shop and said, "That's your supper bell. If you want supper, you better run."

Crevice 22

I didn't know if I should run to the dorm or the Mission House. I picked the Mission House. Then I saw the others marching down from my dorm, and a second bell rang. I was pretty sure I'd made the wrong choice. Much longer lines of Diné students marched from the big gray dorms on either side of the schoolhouse.

After supper Miss Van got out a carom board, and Jessie and a boy named Bobby, whom I recognized as a third grader from my classroom, taught me how to play. While we shot the wooden rings into pockets, two sisters from Naschitti who were in high school took turns practicing the piano. Three high school boys and Wilma did homework in the dining room. "Maybe it won't be so bad," I thought.

Then Miss Van told us it was time for us younger kids to get ready for bed. Bobby went to his room, and Jessie, Bonnie and I headed downstairs. I had brand new flannel pajamas, white with little orange and turquoise stars, ordered from the Sears catalog. I felt I was going to cry, so when I pulled the top on, I kept my head inside. I was afraid to let Jessie see.

"Hey. You. Don't start crying now."

I gulped and said, "I'm not." My voice quavered.

"You're on the verge. I can tell."

I pulled my pajama top on the rest of the way and sought refuge under the covers, pulling them close to my face, so I could cry without being heard.

The next day, I found my safe place. It was behind the big gray Girls' Dorm. The Diné girls' dorm. Irma Ahasteen was in fourth grade, too, and I knew her from Beclaibito, the place next to Teec Nos Pos. She drew me into a game of Red Rover. When the first bell for supper sounded, I raced up the hill, so I could march back down with the missionary kids. The Bilagáana missionary kids.

Crevice 23

The first weekend I went home, I begged my parents to let me stay. "You wanted to go," they said. "Now you have to live with your decision." Only when someone else said, years later, "You were only eight years old," did I realize how inappropriate their reasoning had been.

"Can't I stay in the Girls' Dorm instead?" I asked.

"You can't stay there because the Navajo kids can't go home on weekends. You wouldn't like that, would you?"

"Why can't they?"

"If they go home, they might not go to church. We want them to go to church every Sunday."

Later, I would realize that this constituted one rationale for a separate dormitory for missionary kids. Much later, it would occur to me to wonder why the Diné missionary kids didn't live in our dormitory. Surely no one feared that they wouldn't go to church if they went home on the weekends.

At home, my brother Rick and I made what we called *Ps*. We wouldn't say, "Plans" out loud because they were to be kept secret from our parents. The plans were strategies for keeping me from returning to Rehoboth after a weekend home. Our most elaborate P was to dig a large pit, cover it with branches, and hide me in it until it was past time to leave. That way I would miss my ride in the old green Studebaker with the missionary kids from Shiprock.

Every time I went back to school, I spent the first half hour in class sobbing. I tried desperately but failed to stop myself.

Finally, Miss Silversmith would say, "Why don't you go to the office and get a drink of water?" She never sounded impatient with me, only kind, even though I was the only one who went through this Monday after Monday.

It wasn't every Monday. All the other kids in our dorm went home every weekend, and even though

Crevice 24

I had a ride to Shiprock, my parents said that the thirty miles over the dirt road would be too expensive and hard on the car every week. Two round trips would have amounted to a hundred-twenty miles of rough road, but in my mind it was only thirty, and I couldn't understand why they wouldn't want me home every weekend. I was forced to spend alternate weekends with families that lived on the mission compound. Mostly one family, the Van Bovens, where the children repeated Jessie's bullying less overtly. The Van Boven kids teased me about having skipped a grade. They teased me about being homesick. They laughed when I accidentally slipped into what linguists have called *Dummitawry English*—English spoken with a Diné accent. They dished out the meanness of kids who don't want someone else's kid living with them.

More recently, on a rainy day in August 2014, I took the Railrunner to the First Annual Indigenous Fine Art Market in Santa Fe. From the train, I headed for the booth of my long-time friend Ed Singer. After greetings all around and introductions to family members, I walked around the tent, looking at Ed's and his son Monty's paintings. I have always been deeply moved by Ed's work, which combines traditional Diné themes with avant-garde concepts and style. I stopped short in my tour of the booth and stared at a large painting, overcome by the eeriness of it.

The dominant colors are turquoise, rust, and a darkness that is near-black. The painting places the viewer in the interior of a building, looking outward at two open doors. A dark, rusty space separates the doors, and turquoise light streams through both. Exposed pipes of darker turquoise hang above the doors. The door on the left leads to a sloping entryway that disappears beneath a sort of mezzanine guarded by a metal railing. An illuminated orange EXIT sign hangs above the door to the right, and stairs lead from the mezzanine down to that doorway. A visible light source beckons from the upper left corner of the EXIT, making that turquoise brighter than what is seen through the entryway. The interior, despite the turquoise light, is dark and sinister.

I looked at the image for a long time, mesmerized until Ed's life partner, who is White said to me, "It's boarding school."

I gasped and swallowed, and she said, "Everyone who went to boarding school has that reaction." A lump rose in my throat, and tears came to my eyes. I nodded. Despite what she said, I wasn't sure if Sonja knew that I had gone to boarding school. I didn't tell her either.

In so many ways. I would have been happier in the Diné Girls' Dorm, or so I thought. I've learned since then that bullying went on everywhere at Rehoboth. A mission school is no better than any other school in that way. Boarding school is the worst. There is no relief to be had by going home after school. The adult-child ratio in the dormitories is...there is no ratio to speak of. You are on your own.

A Diné friend who went to Rehoboth told me about his first day there. Before taking him to school, Charlie's parents bought him a red toy truck. After they left, he went outside to play with it. Maybe it was a touchstone with home for him, just as the mission pickup had been for me. Larry, a boy who was a few years older than Charlie, sauntered over to him and said, "Gimme that truck."

Charlie said, "It's mine."

"Not anymore."

Charlie told me, "I didn't have an older brother to stick up for me. It was just me. So Larry and another boy tormented me for years until finally I got big enough and mean enough to beat them up. Then it stopped. But it made me a mean person, even on into adulthood. The women I've been close to could tell you that."

My last two years of high school were agony. Five Bilagáana boys, one of them a Van Boven, brutalized me verbally every day. They mocked my voice. They groaned every time I raised my hand to ask a question. They made degrading comments. The trauma was such that I repressed most of what happened from day-to-day, so that now I can barely remember specifics. For years afterwards, I doubted that it had even happened, until one of the boys, by then a man, told a mutual friend how cruel they had been to me. Apparently, he couldn't tell me directly, but the validation was precious.

All of the adults knew what was going on, and not one of them ever interrupted it. Some laughingly went along with it. I had fantasies of doing what Charlie did—beating those boys up, so they had to be carried out of school on stretchers. In the end, I decided that my best strategy was to speak in class only when called on.

Not only did the adults fail to interrupt persecution by other children, some of the grownups were also bullies. I missed fifty-three days of school in fifth grade for minor, mostly manufactured illnesses because I was terrified of our teacher. She would come into the classroom when we were all seated, some of us quietly chatting with each other and yell, "All right, if you're going to be as mean as a horse, I'm going to be as mean as a horse." She ridiculed a boy who wet his pants when she didn't let him go to the bathroom.

The boy who wet his pants was Diné, but I have to say for Miss Douma that she was indiscriminate in her terrorization of the class. One day the doctor's son, who was Bilagáana, was foolish enough to make an impudent comment. Miss Douma walked over to him, yelling. She grabbed his hair and shook him until his desk fell over. I trembled in my seat, and that afternoon I went home and told my mother what had happened.

"She's the teacher," my mother said. I knew then that no one would stand up for us in the face of the tyranny that was practiced at Rehoboth by adults and children alike.

The matron in the Girls' Dorm was even more notorious among students than Miss Douma was. Her nickname was a Navajo one, *Jaadii*, having to do with her thick calves, and she was universally hated.

Ilene Benally was someone I had known since we were both around six. When we lived at Teec Nos Pos, she and I played together in the small canyon below her mother's hogan and in the arroyo across from the mission. She joined our class at Rehoboth when we were in sixth grade, and we graduated high school in our class of sixteen. At the University of New Mexico (UNM), we took some of the same classes and got our degrees while working in the Navajo Reading Study. Later, Ilene and I shared an office in a Native American educational publishing house.

One day at work, while we were eating burritos at our desks, we fell to reminiscing. Ilene had just written a contemporary story about a traditional Diné character. When she told me about it, I was carried back to the red-walled canyon of our childhood.

"Remember when we used to pretend to be Pueblo Indians down there behind your mom's hogan?"

Ilene chuckled. "Yes," she said.

We shifted to talking about Rehoboth. I'd always known that Jaadii was mean, but I'd never heard specific stories. Or maybe I'd suppressed them.

"One time, because the dorm room was so cold, some of us hopped into bed without praying first," Ilene told me. "Jaadii caught us. She made us kneel on those hard wooden floors in our nightgowns for an hour, while she sat in her rocking chair, wrapped in her shawl, drinking a cup of cocoa, and smiling. Two days later, we all had colds. One of us ended up in the hospital with pneumonia."

"Did you tell anyone?"

Ilene looked at me askance. "It wouldn't do any good."

I nodded. Bullying is about power and powerlessness. Bullies feel powerless in some way, in some part of their lives, so they exert power where they can. I learned that the five Bilagáana boys who bullied me were frequently beat up by Diné boys who saw them as privileged, and they were correct in their perception. Charlie, who was tormented by Larry, tormented my younger brother in turn. Jaadii and Miss Douma, as single women, were at the bottom of the mission's adult heap. The Rehoboth pastor snickered about them as "unplucked flowers" and "unclaimed jewels" when he taught us catechism.

After my first year at Rehoboth, our family moved to Gallup, and I became a day student. But, in high school, I was so miserable that at the end of my sophomore year I talked my parents into asking the principal if I could double up on classes and do summer school at Gallup High. I had it all figured out how I could graduate a year early. His response, "There's something lacking in her socially. She needs to be in more after-school activities." Now I see that he was blaming me for the bullying I endured. One of the bullies happened to be his son.

It wasn't as if the school offered such a wide array of activities. With six, soon to be seven younger children at home, transportation between Gallup and Rehoboth was a deciding factor, so the principal and my parents decided that I could become a boarding student. By that time, there was no White missionary kids' dorm, and there was a separate one for high school students, all of whom were Diné with a few Zuni and Hopi students sprinkled in.

I became the first student to racially integrate a dormitory at Rehoboth. Despite the continued bullying by those Bilagáana boys, it would be the happiest year of my time at the mission school. It was also the year that I became deeply, consciously aware of White privilege and racism there. Not long after the school year began, Bilagáana missionaries in the field got wind of the fact that I was staying in the dorm. They were miffed because as members of the General Conference—the local governing body of the Christian Reformed Church's mission in Dinétah, they had had no input into this decision. That was when I finally learned the ostensible rationale for the existence of the racially separate dorms. It was so White children wouldn't be taking the places meant for Native children who needed to be saved. I wondered yet again why the Diné missionary kids hadn't stayed in the Missionary Kids' Dorm. I still didn't have the word *racism* in my vocabulary, but I recognized it for sure.

In 1963, the Red Power Movement was rumbling awake. In six more years, Vine Deloria, Jr. a Standing Rock Sioux, would publish *Custer Died for Your Sins: An Indian Manifesto*. But already in 1964, he had become executive director of the National Congress of American Indians, growing its

Crevice 30

membership from nineteen to 156 tribes. This nascent movement for Native rights had already influenced some of the more vocal Diné missionaries.

The controversy about integrating the dorm was placed on the agenda at the General Conference, and I knew I might be sent back to stay at home. However, in the end, those vocal Diné missionaries won the day, along with some of the White missionaries, including my father. They argued that integrating the dorms was a symbolic gesture of equality, one that could bring more converts into the fold. It was a wise argument, couched as it was in the rhetoric of saving more souls. I was allowed to stay.

Near the end of the year, something happened to validate the Bilagáana missionaries' worst fears. Kee Bitsoi, a Diné student, and I were both working on the laundry detail by then, and, although he was a class behind me, we were in band and choir together. He asked me to go to church with him one Sunday evening. That might not sound like anything that could possibly threaten anyone, but at the mission it amounted to a very public date. It was like a declaration, and many couples who went to church together on Sunday evenings ended up marrying each other.

I heard audible gasps when we walked down the aisle to our pew, but that was nothing compared to what happened afterwards. The high school dorm had a boys' side and a girls' side with a common living room between. We had two house-parents, Mr. and Mrs. Haverdink. Mister had a nickname—*Yogi*—because his long torso, and the way he waddled made him look like the cartoon character Yogi Bear. Mrs. Haverdink was so uninvolved on a day-to-day basis that she didn't merit a nickname.

Yogi walked up to Kee and me after the service with fury that had been building during the whole service. Scarlet faced, he pushed us apart and said, "You go this way," to me, "and you come with me," to

Kee. As he walked away with Kee, I heard him shout, "I thought you were a nice boy until now."

I was shaking when I got back to the dorm, not in righteous anger, which would have been fitting, but in fear.

Yogi had already sent Kee to his room. "Do you want to marry a White boy or don't you?" he shouted at me, so everyone in the living room could hear.

To my everlasting shame, I said nothing. I didn't need to because Yogi kept ranting for another five minutes, but I wished I had shouted, "No!"

He sent me to my room and told me I was grounded for a week, which basically meant I couldn't go to study hall in the high school library at night. It turned out that Kee had been grounded for the next month, and I was again plunged into shame over the unfairness of it.

Nothing ever came of the incident, except that a week later the principal called me into his office. The only words I remember exactly were, "I guess there's been a storm in the teapot over there." Then he said something to the effect that I should ride it out and maybe not do anything like that again. I nodded miserably and kept my true thoughts and feelings to myself.

I was no longer a boarding student the next year, mostly because I could drive by then and had a job at a supermarket in Gallup. But my stay in the dorm had made me acutely aware that something was drastically wrong at Rehoboth. In Church History class, we were assigned a paper about some topic like Martin Luther's ninety-nine theses or the impact of the Gutenberg Bible on Christianity. I got permission to write instead about Rehoboth.

My paper's unwieldy title was "How the Gospel Is Not Presented at Rehoboth Mission." It was replete with examples of oppression, intimidation, privilege, racism and sexism, although I didn't use any of those words. I was developing a social conscience and trying to have an effect on my world in my own way. I think the minister thought he was indulging me in meaningless teenage rebellion by letting me write the paper. Neither he nor anyone else ever talked with me about it. It was as if my attempt to call attention to the wrongs I'd witnessed slipped into an airless void.

Years later, sitting in our shared office, I told Ilene about that paper. She said, "You saw that back then? I didn't even see it until much later."

This is one of the things that happens when you have a foot in both worlds, or when you live in a crack between two worlds. You see things with different eyes. I was always aware, from the day I ran away from the BIA school in Teec Nos Pos, when my mother got the rules changed for me, that my experience of boarding school was both the same and different from what it was for my friends.

All of us still recognize the same boarding school smells and the taste of government commodity foods. Even though I went home for lunch at Teec Nos Pos, commodity foods were once again part of my diet when I attended Rehoboth, both as a day and a boarding student. We can reminisce about the games we played, about our nicknames for teachers and each other. We can tell stories of things we did together and things that happened to us.

I often become a listener rather than a teller of these stories, afraid of appropriating the pain or indignity that belongs to a friend. I cannot yet explain to myself or anyone else how it is that I quantify and qualify and assign value to their suffering and mine. Perhaps the pain cannot be quantified. There is pain in being a representative of the group that colonized, and there is pain in having been colonized. The sources of the pain are different.

I did face the loss of family and home, as my friends did, but it was for a relatively short period of time with breaks in between. My parents could and did exercise agency; my friends' parents most often did not have the same choices. A couple of years ago, my friend Lila, who is one of the most phenomenal teachers I know, told me about attending the big BIA school at Shiprock.

"The administration decided the dorms and classrooms were too crowded," she said. "So they sent some of us students to the school in Teec Nos Pos. Just sent us without letting our parents know. My older brother was still an elementary student. They called him into the office and told him that when our dad came to get us, he had to be the one to explain where I was.

"My dad was a very protective father. First, when he got to the school to take me home for the weekend, he was worried when he couldn't find me. He went to the office, and they called my brother in. He explained to my dad in Navajo. My father was furious."

I know that this did not and would not have happened to White parents whose children attended boarding school.

My friends' culture was ripped away from them; while my culture was being reinforced for me, it was forced on them. All was familiar to me, foreign to them. Winter is the time when sacred Diné stories are told, and games are played. Strict rules prohibit teaching these cultural foundations at other times of the year. This meant that my friends gradually lost their traditional teachings. Ironically, one of my father's interpreters sat with my siblings and me in the evenings after eating supper with us and told us some of the very stories that were being taken from the rightful heirs.

Little is so core to our humanness, our uniqueness, as our mother tongue. That precious essence, Diné bizaad, was systematically suppressed in an effort to remove it entirely, to make everyone English Only. Diné students were punished for using their own language in boarding school; yet I heard it sometimes on the playground. For them. there was the multifaceted and deep grief of language loss and the partial loss of identity that went with it.

For me, there was a different sort of grief around language. Because my friends weren't allowed to speak Diné, I never learned to use it fluently. The most natural way to learn a second language is in a social setting with one's peers. I'm aware of this loss in so many ways—being able to catch only parts of conversations; dreaming in Danish (in which I *am* fluent) and joyously thinking in the dream that I am speaking Diné bizaad with a friend, only to awaken and discover the reality; feeling envious of younger Whites who grew up in the Nation and are fluent in Diné bizaad because language policies had changed by their time. Nevertheless, I am aware that my loss is different from the losses my friends endured.

The traumas inflicted by the boarding school system are generational for Native people. Great-great grandparents of children now in school were taken from their homes to be "Americanized," and their losses are compounded from generation to generation. In the early days, many children died at boarding school of grief or from physical punishment or illness.

Nevertheless, not everyone talks about negative experiences in boarding school. When I asked Lila if she was frightened when she was moved from the Shiprock school to the Teec Nos Pos one, she said, "Oh, no. I was with all my friends. They were like family. And I knew that road. I knew I had relatives there because my dad was from there." To this day, Lila is one of the most positive people I know, always finding the bright side of things but not in a superficial way, so I believed that what she said was genuine.

Not long ago, I attended the funeral of an upperclassman at Rehoboth. I went mainly because I knew one of my classmates would be there. She and I stood outside the church catching up after the service, and, as we stood there, I overheard a classmate of the woman who had died talking about Rehoboth.

"Yeah," she said loudly, "they say we were abused there. I say they abused us pretty good because we're still all part of that church." The women she was talking to laughed with her. I thought she might be carrying a pretty heavy load of denial.

Charlie, on the other hand, has the self-awareness of someone who has done his work and can speak about his experience of boarding school in a balanced way. He talks about the bullying and abuse that was endemic to the system. He talks about the hypocrisy he saw in the missionaries. But he also says that he is grateful for the excellent academic education he received. "I can speak articulately and think critically, and I got that there—at Rehoboth," he says.

A few weeks ago, I got an email from my friend Alice Whitegoat. She attended Rehoboth about ten years before I did. Alice wrote that her niece had been at the Indian Health Hospital in Shiprock. "My niece saw this woman we know. The woman was so thin and wasted. Her hair had gone completely white, and she was barely able to walk without assistance."

This friend had attended Rehoboth, too, and, until recently, had been a strong presence in Navajo education. "She told my niece that she was suffering, but she couldn't remember what her illness was called. She turned to her husband to ask him. 'Depression,' he told her. She started to cry. She said she can't stop crying."

Alice asked me, "Is that a Rehoboth disease?"

I wanted to cry.

Crevice 36

I don't forget Ed's painting. I imagine small Diné children lined up, marching in and down that ramp that looks like a livestock chute. I imagine teenagers marching down the steps, back into the light, forever changed. And I imagine myself standing in that dark, rusty space between the two doors.

Some Things Were True

> "We die containing a richness of lovers
> and tribes, tastes we have swallowed,
> fears we have hidden in as if caves."
> ~Michael Ondaatje, *The English Patient*

I shivered when I walked among the graves across the road from the mission. We had to pass through that dry, rocky cemetery with its weathered wooden crosses and sun-bleached plastic flowers on our way to the top of the massive golden mesa beyond it. The graves were pocked with small holes dug by mice and gophers, maybe even snakes. I was afraid I would see part of a dead body, a bony hand reaching out of a hole, a grinning skull, if I looked into one. I felt a sick looseness in my throat when I thought of little animals living down there with decaying bodies.

In the small valley of Teec Nos Pos in Dinétah, my father was Éé'nishoodii Yázhí, Little Long Coat— the Protestant missionary, as differentiated from the Catholic fathers with their long robes. Whenever we came into Teec Nos Pos from the east, we drove down a sharp incline to enter the valley. At the bottom of the hill, I couldn't help seeing the charred, broken timbers of a ch'íidii baghan that stood there. I asked my father once about its name, and he said, "It means *ghost house*. People call it that because someone died in there. Navajos are afraid to live in it after that because they're afraid of death. They break a hole in the north side of the hogan for the person's spirit to leave. Then they burn it. It's such a sad waste of a good home when people are so poor. We want them to know they don't need to fear death because Jesus gives us victory over death through his resurrection."

I nodded. I believed that everything he told me was true. And I shivered then, too, even though I also believed I should have no reason to fear death. In my mind's eye, I watched frightened people breaking a hole in the back wall of the hogan and then setting their shelter on fire. Chills moved up my spine. I wouldn't go near a ch'íidii baghan myself, if I could help it. I didn't want to see or touch people who were dead any more than the Diné did.

Because he believed they were terrified of death, my father also believed that the greatest service he could offer Diné people was helping them bury their dead. He and my mother washed and dressed bodies; Dad built pine boxes, dug graves, and spoke words. I don't know how much comfort he gave because he also believed that he must preach the gospel at every opportunity. Unsaved people might be standing around the grave, and it was his mission to bring them to Christ, even if that meant scaring them with stories of hell awaiting them after death.

One evening at dinner, my father said something to my mother that got my attention. "We were burying that Benally man this afternoon. I got him washed and dressed, and had the box made."

It was his tone that made me look up. I saw his half-smile, which meant he was trying to suppress some emotion. I could tell he didn't want to be smiling, but he couldn't help it.

His voice cracked. "The body wouldn't fit in the coffin. It was too tall. I measured him, but I must've gotten something wrong. I took his shoes off, and that helped, but he was still too tall." Dad laughed, a helpless laugh. "After that I tried to bend his feet back."

By then I sensed that my father's laughter was about to cross over into something else.

"I was afraid I was going to break his legs," he said. "Finally I got the corpse stuffed into the box." At last, he stopped laughing and seemed relieved.

My mother did not laugh. She looked sympathetic. I looked at my father in wonder, feeling that something in him had come close to breaking, if only for a moment.

All I could think about was his hands touching that dead body—*corpse* he called it. He had touched death that afternoon. My throat underwent that same loosening I felt when I walked through the graveyard. I wanted my father to wash his hands with the gritty gray Lava soap he used whenever he changed the oil in the pickup, the soap that made his hands feel smooth and smell clean. I wanted him to wash them a second time before I would let him touch me.

The night of the too-long body, my father had a dream. He told it to us at breakfast the next morning. "That Benally man sat up in his coffin just after I got him crammed in," he said. He licked his dry lips and started laughing all over again.

I could tell it was a scary dream. Maybe that was the first time I wondered if it was true that Christians didn't fear death.

Sometime later, my dad said that he would become a mortician if he ever stopped being a missionary. That is how great a service he believed he was performing when he buried the Diné dead.

I shuddered. I knew that if he handled death every day, he would never be able to wash it off. "If you become a mortician," I said, "I won't ever let you touch me again."

He laughed. "You'd get used to it," he said.

I didn't believe it.

On a sunny spring morning when I was seven or eight, my mother called me away from the game I was playing with my brothers and sister by the side of the house. "I want to show you something," she said.

She led me into my father's study in the small building between our house and the chapel. It was always cool in there, unless the tall blue kerosene heater was lit. The room smelled of Bible leather and the musty yellow paper of commentaries and concordances, of mahogany and cracked linoleum.

On that day, I noticed another faint, slightly sweet smell mingling with and rising above the old familiar smells. On the desk where my father prepared his sermons, a Diné baby girl lay on her wooden cradleboard. She wore a traditional, dark green velveteen skirt and blouse with a turquoise and silver pin at her throat, delicate bracelets on her wrists and tiny black patent leather shoes on her feet. Her eyes were closed, and her face was pale, a kind of milky beige, surrounded by fine dark brown hair. Her cheeks were round and fat.

"Isn't she beautiful? We wanted you to see her because she's so beautiful," my mother said. "So peaceful."

"Are you going to show her to the other kids?"

"They're too young to understand."

I was torn between pride that I was old enough and not wanting to be that old. I thought the little girl looked stiff and too pale for a Diné baby. Not beautiful.

My mother closed the door to the study and headed for the house. I stood a moment longer in the shadow of the study, then took off running up the hill behind the mission, leaping over stones like the curly-haired goats I sometimes herded with my friends. I could hear the voices of my brothers and sister from among the juniper bushes, and I wanted to find them, to return to the game that had moved on a ways while I witnessed death.

I didn't expect death to taste like anything, but it did. When I was twelve, my only sister, Trudy, was diagnosed with leukemia. While she was sick, I spent hours on the terminal pediatrics ward, massaging her feet and legs because they were wracked with pain caused by the changes in her bone marrow. One by one, other children disappeared from the ward. Trudy died two weeks before my thirteenth birthday. We drove to Michigan to bury her next to my grandmother, and at the funeral home I stood with my parents by her coffin. All the time we stood there, an acrid smell floated above the over-sweetness of the formal bouquets.

After the visitation, we went to my uncle and aunt's house for supper. My aunt had made a fruit salad, and the mayonnaise on the silver-plate serving spoon recreated that smell, a deathly sharpness mixed with sweetness.

"It smells like the funeral home," I said.

The adults said, "It does not. It's all in your head. Don't be silly."

I knew my parents were embarrassed by my impoliteness. But I couldn't eat the salad.

I didn't want to go to the funeral. I'd had enough of death after the visitation. But my mother said I had to. "You'll be sorry later if you don't."

So I went, and I cried the whole time, which was probably good for me. I wore my royal blue pleated wool skirt and vest and a long-sleeved white cotton blouse. Those clothes should have been too hot in May, but I shivered.

Trudy wore the prettiest dress I'd ever owned. It didn't come from a mission barrel or a catalog. My mother had sewn it for my piano recital a year and a half earlier—pink and white organdy with little rosebuds. I felt scared when I imagined what would be happening to my dress and Trudy's body inside the coffin. In the ground.

Beside the grave, relatives and friends hugged my parents. I stood there, not knowing what to do. Because we were in Michigan, John Tsosie, one of my father's former interpreters, was the only Diné present. He was also the only person who noticed that, although I was a child, I was grieving, too. He was the only one who came over to me and hugged me long and hard and cried with me. He looked into my eyes, and our eyes were like round baskets, pouring our grief back and forth.

Afterwards there was food again—ham on rolls, milk with cream on top from my grown-up cousin's farm, salads. I didn't eat any of it. The funeral smell hung in my nostrils, and I couldn't get rid of it. I couldn't eat mayonnaise after that for a long time because it tasted like death. When it sits on a silver-plate spoon, mayonnaise turns green.

In the months after Trudy's death, dreams kept waking me. My armpits prickled with ice, and fear lay in my stomach. I'd get up and sit on the porch in my pajamas and wait for the sun to come up. In my dreams, my dead grandmother sat up in her coffin. Or Trudy came back for a visit. We'd be talking or playing, and I'd be so glad to see her. Then all of a sudden I'd realize, "She's not supposed to be here. She's supposed to be dead." Only I couldn't tell her because, while she was sick, I wasn't supposed to tell her she was dying. My gladness chilled to fear. I didn't want to be around this dead person, my little sister, and I needed to figure out how I could get away without her suspecting anything. I needed to tell my parents she was back, so they could tell her she was dead, so she would go back to where she belonged.

I told my mother and father about my dreams. They said, "You don't need to be afraid. Trudy's safe with Jesus now."

I was the one who felt unsafe.

I'm not sure why the idea of the dead coming back to life is so frightening. In our imaginations, they don't come back truly alive but as the living dead, zombies. The notion defies a most basic natural law.

In my late teens and early twenties, I worked in the mission hospital as a nursing assistant. I often worked nights, and it was my task at the beginning of each shift to make rounds of the thirty-bed hospital to see if the patients were sleeping or if they needed anything. That's how I happened to find old Mr. Arviso after he died.

I walked into the men's ward, which had six beds, and in the bed farthest from the door, I noticed that this big, barrel-chested man had removed his hospital gown. Then I saw that his chest wasn't rising and falling. My heart squeezed and rose to my throat, and I watched for a moment longer to make sure he wasn't breathing. I didn't check his pulse but left quickly to find the registered nurse.

Ruth came back with me and after checking his pulse, confirmed my observation. We pulled the curtain around his bed and brought in a gurney. I asked Ruth, "Do I have to touch him?"

"No," she said. "We can use his sheet to lift him onto the stretcher."

The morgue, like all hospital morgues, lay in the basement. But the mission hospital had no elevators, and we had to roll the gurney down a gravelly incline, scored by sizeable ruts from recent rains. There were no outside lights, and it was a moonless night. Although we had strapped the body to the stretcher, gravity and the man's weight caused it to tilt to the side, threatening to tip the gurney off its wheels. Ruth and I giggled, and soon my laughter bordered on hysteria. It was like my father's nervous laughter when he couldn't get that corpse to fit into the box.

Once we'd gotten the body into the morgue, we went about our routines. Ruth went into the newborn nursery to feed babies. I went to the children's ward to make prescribed formulas. Then I powdered rubber gloves and folded them into cloth wrappers so they could be put into the autoclave, sterilized and reused. All night my skin tingled with heightened awareness, and every time I looked in on a patient, it was with the expectation that they might have died since the last time I checked.

Around three o'clock, Ruth and I sat down to eat in the windowed corner of the kitchen. Night blackness pressed on the panes. Ruth faced the hallway, and I gazed at the windows. Suddenly, she gasped. I jerked, and panic flooded my body.

"What?" I heard the alarm in my voice. I was afraid to turn toward the hallway.

"I forgot to put the nursery bottles into the sterilizer."

I stared at her as my panic decelerated. "That's it?" I said. "I thought Mr. Arviso came back to life and was walking down the hall." We both laughed, but I decided I'd had enough to eat.

Every death I witnessed in the hospital became a little easier, and it wasn't long before I was able to bathe a body, still lying in its bed, to do the work my mother and father used to do when someone died. I still felt unusually alert, though, always aware of the mystery I attended. I felt that anything could happen, that I understood so little about this crossing over. When a body, sometimes hours after death, exhaled for the last time, I startled. It was as if the flesh had

Crevice 45

heaved a great sigh. My old fear returned momentarily—fear of the dead coming back.

It was my father who taught me to speak my first Diné words. He taught me how to read in the Diné language at the same time I was learning to read English. This was at a time when a minuscule number of people, Diné or Bilagáana, knew how to read in Diné bizaad. From my father, I also learned something of Diné beliefs. Many of them were ones he'd learned from other White men. For a long time, I believed that what he told me was the way it was.

When I began having adult relationships with adult Diné, I started to see traditional beliefs in a different light. Often, I was astounded. At one point, I taught an introductory psychology class for Diné College. Except for a Lakota man, all of my students were Diné. In addition to a standard general psychology text, each week I assigned a chapter from Carl Hammerschlag's *The Dancing Healers*. Carl had both learned from and helped Native patients, healers, and leaders in his practice of psychiatry with the Indian Health Service. I used his book because I wanted to affirm the idea that a Eurocentric approach to psychology is not the only way to look at the human mind. Through story and reflection, Carl offered a unique perspective. I also encouraged my students to bring in speakers from the community to broaden viewpoints about the human condition.

I assigned one chapter from *The Dancing Healers* for its wonderful description of neurosis. The words came from a Mojave Indian father, speaking to his daughter about some problems she was having in college. He compared the problems to a hardening Jell-O mold, saying "You [cannot] ignore the forces of darkness, or they [will] harden you." I thought the selection would help us connect with the chapter in the psychology text on so-called abnormal behavior, including neuroses. We spoke a little about the Mojave man's definition, comparing it with what the students had read in the text. Then we spent most of the next two and a half hours talking about cultural customs surrounding death. In the story, the young Mojave woman eventually died, and the family had held a traditional Mojave cremation ceremony.

A woman in the class spoke up, "Our people used to cremate bodies. They burned them in the hogan they died in, and then the hogan was respected as their place. The spirit was gone on to another life, but we stayed away from the house out of respect for them and for the place that was theirs now. Also, as a way of letting them go."

My mind whirled back to the burned hogan at the base of the mesa in Teec Nos Pos. I knew immediately that my student was describing a ch'íidii baghan, but what she said about it bore almost no resemblance to what my father had told me all those years earlier. Goose bumps peppered my arms.

The student went on talking. "But when you go to a funeral at a cemetery, people just walk all over the place, showing no respect for the bodies of the people there."

Another student spoke up, "Some of us walk around among the dead because we're Christian. I was raised Christian, not traditional Navajo, and Christians don't fear death. We aren't afraid to be near those bodies. We don't have all those taboos about the dead."

Internally, my eyes widened. At that moment, I could have been back in our 1953 Chevy sedan, riding down the side of the mesa and asking my father about the ch'íidii baghan. This young Diné man could have been my father. He didn't hear the woman who had spoken first. He didn't hear that she said nothing about fear, only about respect. The missionaries had taught him, as my father taught me, that the

Crevice 47

observances around ch'íidii baghan were about fear of death. The student believed that fear came from not having the comfort of Christianity. His Christian-tinted glasses kept him from seeing it any other way.

In those few minutes of discussion, I learned a lot about my father and other Christian missionaries. I thought that if they saw how similar some Navajo beliefs were to their own, they might discover there was little need to convert people. Both believed that the spirit of the dead person went on to another life. Both traditional Diné and Christians believed that the final resting place should be respected. Both believed they needed to let go of the person who had died, trusting that the spirit was still alive. Maybe missionaries had a need to see Diné beliefs and customs around death as fearful, requiring the comfort of salvation, in order to make their task essential.

I wondered if missionaries might have projected some of their own fears about death and dying onto Diné beliefs. I remembered hearing the Bilagáana missionary's wife at Naschitti tell a scary local ghost story—a story she obviously believed. I'd heard as many or more of those stories from White Christians as I had from traditional Diné. I didn't have much confidence anymore in people who claimed to have no fear of death simply because of what they believed—whether it was because Jesus took away the sting of death or because, in the Diné Way, death might be seen as an ordinary aspect of life.

But I also knew Bilagáana traders, who had no interest in converting anyone, tell how traditional Navajos fear the dead. I've heard the same thing from non-Christian Diné, too. "There's so much fear in traditional religion," they say. "Fear of the dead" they add to a list of prohibitions.

Maybe fearing the dead and death is just a part of life that we all brush up against at one time or another. Maybe no one can generalize, as my father and other White missionaries and anthropologists did, "Navajos believe this about death." Or that. There is no reason to think that all traditional Diné believe the same thing about anything, any more than all Christians hold to uniform beliefs.

I find it easiest to trust people who admit they have known both—the fear and the naturalness of death. I imagine that even when they have released their fear, it comes back at times, that we need to confront such a great mystery, such an unknown, more than once in a lifetime. That was true for me, as I went from fearing that old Mr. Arviso would get up from his gurney, trudge up the graveled hill, and stalk down the hallway into the kitchen, to being able to bathe and dress patients who had just died. Later on, I could even be present with someone at their crossing over.

In April of 2008, my mother called early in the morning before I could leave for work. "Your daddy's gone to Glory," she said. She had never before called him *your daddy*. Not to me. It felt odd. Later, I remembered that she and her sisters never stopped calling my grandfather *Daddy*. But I had stopped calling my father *Daddy* years earlier. People do and say things they otherwise wouldn't when someone has just died. It *was* like my mother to say he'd "gone to Glory," in a rare moment of allowing herself to be dramatic.

I called in to work after talking with my mother and drove to Gallup, 136 miles from where I lived. I needed to see my father before the morticians got their hands on him. I went straight to the mortuary, and they told me they wouldn't let me see him, that I wouldn't want to, until they fixed him up. I went outside, sat on a bench in the sun and cried. Not from grief, probably not even so much because I needed that time with him, but from a feeling of powerlessness. The funeral director saw me and had a change of heart. She took me to a small room where my father lay on a gurney, zipped up to his hands and chest in a plastic, navy blue body bag. His mouth gaped, I suppose in his last gasp for air, but his eyes were closed.

I touched my father's bony hands. They were cold. I sat by his side and told him things I hadn't been able to tell him when his mind had left him or before that when he was so angry with me for not following his path. I told him, "Thank you for taking care of me. Thank you for teaching me that there is a life of the spirit. Thank you for teaching me to read the Diné language when I was starting to read English. Thank you for telling me about Diné life as you believed it was. I'm sorry we couldn't talk better with each other at the end. I love you, Dad." I cried a little but not a lot, and then I left and went to see my mother.

She was baffled when I told her I'd been to see my dad and how difficult it had been just to be allowed to see him. "Why did you think you needed to see him that way anyway? And why did you need to go by yourself?"

I thought if I had to explain it, she probably wouldn't understand, so I let her questions lie between us.

Three days later, we all went to the funeral home and had family time with my dad in the pine coffin my brothers had built. The mortician had sewn Dad's lips shut. He couldn't yell at me anymore to tell me that on Judgment Day I would pray for the rocks and the mountains to fall on me. He didn't look like himself, either, with his lips that way.

That evening, in my mother's living room we gathered—children, grandchildren, nieces, and nephews—and told stories about my dad. We talked about how he always pulled a comb out of his back pocket to slick back his hair when he was walking

Crevice 50

from the car to a store or church; how he would spin a car full of us kids on ice; how he loved to take a handful of sage leaves, rub them and hold them out to us and say, "Smell!" We laughed and ate sweets and talked about the sweetness of the man and the traits we had inherited from him.

Many Diné came to my father's funeral. John Tsosie, who comforted me at Trudy's funeral, drove five hours each way to be present. Christian converts came to Gallup from as far away as Teec Nos Pos and Albuquerque. In the graveyard, a hole had been dug in what is known as *Missionary Row*. Old missionaries, dating back to a death date of 1936, lie next to each other. My brothers and I lowered the coffin on ropes. One of my brothers pointed out that I seemed to be in a rush because my end was dropping too fast. Maybe I just wasn't as strong as them. And maybe I was in a rush.

Sharla, the daughter of one of the converts from Teec Nos Pos, was someone I knew pretty well, a PhD psychologist. Several shovels stood in the pile of earth beside the grave, and we were told that anyone could scoop in some dirt. Sharla grabbed a spade before anyone else and energetically tossed in several shovelfuls. She is generally a vigorous woman, but one of my brothers and I both noticed that she seemed eager. We wondered if she were getting some kind of closure. We didn't think she'd known Dad that well. Maybe it was closure with all the Bilagáana missionaries she'd known.

It is a cliché that your life changes in unforeseen ways when a parent dies because a generation no longer stands between you and death as a sort of buffer. I didn't believe my dad's death would affect me that way, but for a long time after that, hardly a day went by that I didn't think about my own mortality. For one thing, I am closer now to my death than to my birth. I think to myself, "I'm going to die someday. How can that be? How will it happen?

Crevice 51

When? Fast or slow? What will the days before it be like?"

Fear of the dead, which later became fear of dying, rarely accompanies my thoughts. It does visit now and then, though only briefly. Most of the time, I am struck with a sense of wonder, of incomprehension. I cannot imagine a world where I am not. This is not because I think I am indispensable but because this is the only place I have known myself to *be*. Even the certainty of death is incomprehensible. It *will* happen.

Death has changed, or I have changed in relationship to it. At times I wonder how my thoughts about death may morph yet again, whether I might be granted some understanding of it before it happens to this body I call *me*. Mostly I am simply in awe of the mystery of it, which I suppose is what that fear disguised all along.

In the Girls' Room

Janice Becenti must have been waiting for me to come out of my stall in the girls' dorm bathroom at the Rehoboth Mission School because she came out of hers right after me. It was morning recess, and we were the only two in there.

Janice was a big girl, bigger than me anyhow, and Diné to my Bilagáana. She was in sixth grade; I was in fifth, and we shared a classroom. Her father was a missionary near Crownpoint, and mine was the missionary at Tohlakai at the time. Janice had never paid much attention to me, but I couldn't help feeling a little bit scared of her. She looked me in the eye that day and, seemingly out of nowhere, said, "You know, the Navajo people really like your dad, but they don't like your mother very much." With that she flounced into the room with the long porcelain trough. I watched our soapy water mix and run down the rust-red stripe toward the drain. The water at the mission tasted of salt and iron.

I didn't say anything to Janice to defend my mother, even though she was still the most important person in my life then. She was the person I talked with more than anyone else. I didn't say anything to Janice, not because I wasn't loyal to my mother. I was. It was because I was pretty sure I understood what Janice meant. I even thought she was probably right, and in that moment, I felt sad about my mother. I could have wondered where Janice had gotten this information, but I didn't.

When my mother died four days before her hundredth birthday, our family waited a few months to hold her memorial because of the pandemic. That months-long wait could explain why so few Diné people joined us in celebration of her life. A week or so after we buried her ashes, I had a long conversation with my cousin Cor. She asked me, "How come there were hardly any Navajos at the memorial? I mean, it was in the same church as your dad's funeral, and probably more than half the people at his were Navajo. I could count Navajos on one hand at your mom's."

"You're right," I said. "My dad's funeral was a great reunion with people I hadn't seen for years. After I talked with everyone there, the only food left at the reception was a slice of banana bread. Which I hate." I laughed. And then I suggested that the long wait between Mom's death and the memorial might have had something to do with how few Diné people joined us. "But there's more, I think."

There was a lot more.

I had felt agitated in the days after the memorial, and Cor's question was what I needed to talk about. People expect us to say good things about the dead at a funeral. If I'm asked to speak, I try to say interesting things, things that will give people a glimpse of sides they may not have known about the person. We had divided my mother's eulogy into three parts because one hundred years is a lot of time to cover. I didn't say anything bad about my mother, but I was careful not to heap praise on her either. There were people who did that. One of my brothers spoke several times about how hospitable my mother had been to Diné people. To my ears, what he said amounted to glorification. The implication was that there was something magnanimous about her, and there was an us-them quality to the words that made my skin crawl.

Within a couple of days of the funeral, some truth-telling took place on social media. My nephew Noah posted a nuanced entry about my parents' missionary life. He wrote about how their good intentions and perhaps naïveté had been destructive to a Diné way of life and about how that had been omitted from the memorial speeches. I was grateful to Noah. What he did took integrity and courage. He described my parents' role within the post-colonial system—the way churches and government worked together hand-in-glove to change the Indigenous way of life, to effect assimilation.

But he necessarily left out the specifics that might answer Cor's question about my mother. Because he was of the next generation, he didn't know things I knew, things even my younger siblings don't know. To Noah, my mother had been the grandma who looked after him and his brother and sister after school, supplied them with cookies, and put bandaids on their owies.

I hadn't thought about that moment in the Girls' Room with Janice Becenti for years. Noah's post and Cor's question put me back there, and Janice became part of the story I told to Cor.

My mother had decided when she was eight years old that she wanted to be a medical missionary, and after high school she trained to be a registered nurse. After nursing school, she applied to our church's mission board to go to China, but the revolution was in progress there, and China was evicting missionaries, not taking in new ones. Her next choice was Nigeria, but there was going to be a delay in sending her, and the board asked if, while she waited, she'd like to go to the mission hospital at Rehoboth, New Mexico, which served the Navajo Nation.

I've never thought of my mother as especially adventuresome, but being a missionary in a foreign country could be a path to the exotic for a single young woman of my mother's generation and conservative religious background. She was reared with an intense obligation to convert people to Christianity. She embraced the assumption that non-White people in other countries—people of other cultures, anyone seen as Other—needed salvation. Christian duty, not the allure of the unusual, was probably the main motivation for her life choice.

Missionary stories were a staple in my childhood reading. There were tales of single missionary women riding bicycles through the perilous savannah of East Africa. They learned what to me were exotic languages and lived in grass huts shared with snakes and rats. There were women who decided to carry on alone when their missionary husbands were murdered by people who didn't want what they had to offer. Clearly, many women of the past and of my mother's own generation had pursued more than duty; they were also drawn to the romance of the unknown when they set out as missionaries.

The appeal of risk and adventure seems more theoretical when it comes to my mother, since she never appeared to be particularly curious about Diné ways. She accepted what other Bilagáana missionaries told her. In general, she was a follower of rules. What she thought was most often something she had received from others. It wasn't that my mother wasn't intelligent, but she wasn't a critical thinker. She had grown up with an overly developed acceptance of authority.

Even if it was duty, not risk or adventure, that attracted my mother to the missionary life, she was quite capable of being intrepid in the face of danger.

One Sunday, when she had stayed home in Teec Nos Pos with the little ones, my dad and us older children went off to church services in Beclabito, seven miles away over a dirt road. My mother had put the children down for a nap, then walked over to the chapel to make things ready for the afternoon church service there. Someone had left a bunch of toys on the wooden steps leading to the front door. She bent to pick them up and came face to face with a coiled rattlesnake. For some reason the snake had not sounded its warning. My mother backed off, hands no doubt trembling, and went back to the house for a shovel. She hurried back to the chapel and found that the rattler had not moved. She lofted the shovel and decapitated the snake, wiped her sweaty palms onto her apron, then went about the rest of her morning.

Diné people might not have liked my mother, but quite a few came to trust her as a nurse, and when she was called on in that capacity, she was always ready to serve. When she was offered Navajo Country as a temporary substitute for Nigeria, my mother agreed and took her first airplane ride to the Rehoboth Mission Hospital, five miles east of Gallup. It was 1946, and she met my father at the mission. He arrived after her by a few months to work as the cook for the boarding school and hospital, having learned institutional cooking in the Army during the war. They married in 1947 and drove to Michigan, so he could attend Bible School and become a Bible-preaching missionary instead of a cooking one. I think they had always hoped to return to Dinétah. By the time the mission board sent them in 1952, they had three children, of whom I was the eldest, nearly four years old.

Over the years, I saw things my mother did for which Diné people could have loved her. And maybe they did sometimes. One Sunday, after the morning church service, someone came to the interpreter who worked with my father and told him a baby had been born the night before and was very sick. Could my mother come to the family hogan to see him? We drove over, and my mother stooped to enter the traditional earthen home. She was in there only a few minutes when she came back out, walking swiftly and carrying a small bundle wrapped in a blanket.

My father turned the car around, and we headed for Shiprock, where there was an Indian Health Service hospital. From the back seat, I watched my mother hold the tiny, naked, wrinkled baby upside down by his ankles. His skin, which should have been a rich brown, was blue-gray. Periodically my mother thumped his back, and she kept wiping him down with a wet cloth.

"Why are you holding him that way?" I asked.

"He's barely breathing because there's mucus in his air passages. If I had a bulb syringe, I could suck some of it out. Holding him upside down helps drain the fluid, so he can breathe easier. He has a high fever. That's why I'm using this wet cloth. I'm trying to bring the fever down."

The car bumped over the dusty, rock-strewn road. My father didn't watch out for rocks the way he usually did. We jerked over them, going faster than we ever had.

At the hospital, my mother rushed in with the baby. Hardly any time passed before she came back without him. "They said his temperature went all the way up to the end of the thermometer. Probably past it," she said. She sounded so serious, so worried. "They don't know if he's going to make it."

The boy did live and got named Clifford. The doctors said my mother had saved his life. Clifford grew brown and chubby, and whenever we saw him, his family called him my mother's baby. Surely, that was a kind of love.

Crevice 58

Still, it's not difficult for me to see why my mother was not liked in the same way my dad was. Her own mother was a brusque, direct woman, quick to judge, and she included my mother in her pronouncements. There never seemed to be room for doubt about what Grandma thought of people and their foibles. Once in my mother's kitchen, I was a silent witness to one of her cruel comments. By that time my mother had given birth to nine children (her mother had had only three), and my mom said something about the joys and maybe even the religious obligation to bring children into the world. Grandma said, without pause, "Yes, but a woman is not a cow, for instance." I almost laughed, but I saw my mother's face and bit my lips.

Despite, or more likely because of, having absorbed many more belittlements and perhaps worse, my mother became a judgmental person herself. If she didn't come right out and say what she was thinking, and she usually did, at least at home, her attitudes were communicated by her stern visage.

There was a bit more to the rattlesnake story. Before my mother went for the shovel, she noticed that there was a Navajo Police vehicle parked up the hill at the Bureau of Indian Affairs school. She went back to the house and called the school, which, since it was a boarding school, was staffed on Sundays. She asked to speak to the officer. She wanted him to kill the snake for her. When she told us the story at dinner, she said, "He hemmed and hawed, said maybe, and I knew he wasn't going to do it. What a chicken."

My father said, "But you know Navajo people aren't supposed to have anything to do with snakes."

"Yes, but he's a policeman," she said. "Why be a policeman if you're afraid of a snake? If you can't help people who need help? Those Navajo Police are useless."

My mother raised us the way she was raised—— not to question authority; it didn't even occur to me to have an opinion about what my mother had just said. Though I had no opinion then, clearly my mother's blatant othering, made an impression, as I stored this and similar incidents. They would lie at the root of my radically opposing views later on.

Old Lady Appel was thin and bent and moved swiftly down the dusty road in front of the mission whenever she came by. No one seemed to know where her name came from, though her face did have as many wrinkles as the skin of an apple ready for the compost. Her long skirts swished around her high-top work boots, and her cane barely touched the ground. "What does she carry that cane for?" my mother complained. "Obviously she doesn't need it, walking at that clip. She's practically running."

When Old Lady Appel turned off the road and onto the mission compound, my mother groaned. "Why does she always have to come here when we're eating? And when you're home for once?" That was addressed to my father, who was rarely home at lunchtime.

Sometimes it was a mystery why Old Lady Appel came at all, and contrary to my mother's complaint, it wasn't always at lunch. I thought she was the oldest person I knew, and I can still see her sitting on the kitchen floor, even though she'd been offered a chair, while my mother, who probably spent more time in the kitchen than in any other room, worked at the sink. Neither spoke each other's language, though I could sometimes hear the old woman rattling on at my mother in Diné bizaad. It was almost as if she thought my mother would grasp what she was saying if she just kept on talking long enough.

When I look back, I think Old Lady Appel's visits might even have been a form of hospitality. Possibly she thought my mother must be lonely—a Bilagáana woman in Dinétah without her extended family nearby. Or maybe the old lady was just out walking and wanted the cup of water she knew my mother would offer.

I try to understand my mother's antipathy, which descended to its nadir when it came to Old Lady Appel but was often present when other Diné people showed up unannounced. Although she was a guest in their land, my mother's attitude reflected the US government's post-colonial assimilation policies of the 1950s. I often heard her refer to "those people," resentment in her voice, for many reasons, one of them because "they" had not adopted the White habit of arranging a visit ahead of time. It was an empty, ridiculous wish, as only the trading post, the school, and the mission had telephones, which made pre-arranged visits an impossibility. Never mind that scheduled visits weren't part of the Diné hospitality culture.

Aside from her insensitivity to the host culture at best and her racism at worst, I know my mother lived under constant stress. While we lived at Teec Nos Pos, her passel of children doubled to six; in the summer we had electricity only two hours a day in the evenings; her hands were always red and cracked from laundering clothes on a washboard and in a wringer washer—including piles of cloth diapers— and from hanging them outdoors to dry in all weathers; she accompanied church services (sometimes three on a Sunday) on the piano, pump organ, or accordion. But chief among her grievances was the fact that my father was absent far more than she thought necessary.

He was gone to passionately spread the gospel. And to help people—probably one explanation for the first half of Janice Becenti's pronouncement: "You know, the Navajo people really like your dad."

One day my mother's nemesis did come by when we were eating lunch, on a day when my father happened to be home. We saw her scuttling along the road, turning in at the mission. My mother had things to say from the moment she saw the woman. When Old Lady Appel knocked at the back door—the only door we used—my father went to answer. A few minutes later, he came back. "I need to get John's help," he said. "She keeps mentioning łį́į́', her horse. She's making the motions of throwing up and holding her nose, but I can't put together what she's talking about."

The interpreter's house was a few hundred yards from ours, and my father went to get Mr. Tsosie, who was doubtless also eating lunch. Together they talked with Old Lady Appel. Then Dad came back and said he had to go out to her place. "Her horse died a few days ago, and the smell is so bad, it's making her sick. She hasn't eaten for three days."

He knew my mother would object, and she did. "Can't you at least finish your lunch first? That horse isn't going anywhere." But he put on his fedora, which I suppose looked odd with his short-sleeved, white nylon shirt and khaki pants with the front pleats. He left in the mission pickup with Mr. Tsosie and Old Lady Appel.

Over dinner that night, he told us the story. "She was right, you know. The smell was so terrible, John and I had a hard time not vomiting. We threw a couple old tires on top of the horse, and some gas, and started the pile on fire. The burning rubber smelled terrible, too, but it got rid of the decaying horse smell. If we had just burned the horse, the stink would've hung around."

"Wasn't there anyone else around there who could help her?"

"She asked us," Dad said.

"Well, I hope she was thankful."

"She didn't say anything about that." He grinned.

"Of course not."

In the early part of the 20th century, progressive Christians promoted the Social Gospel Movement, which they saw as living into what Jesus preached in his Sermon on the Mount—not just taking his words as nice ideas. To them, it meant actually feeding the poor, bringing clean water to countries where people were dying for lack of it. It meant sharing the love they believed was the essence of Christianity in concrete ways. If that drew people to becoming Christians, well and good, but proselytizing was not their goal.

Evangelical Christians like my parents disparaged the Social Gospel; they believed the people they called *liberals* (progressive Christians) were taking an easy path, substituting the Social Gospel for preaching. The battle against liberals was almost as strong as the battle against Satan. They went so far as to say that liberals were not really Christians. My father talked about the Social Gospel pretty often, always with a sneer. And yet, in many ways he practiced it alongside his preaching by doing things like burning a dead horse, so an old woman could eat.

My father was not a saint in the conventional meaning of the word. He could have put his wife first on the day of the dead horse and sat at the table for another fifteen minutes before heading out to stack tires on the corpse. It would've been a loving thing to do and wouldn't have asked much of him.

On the other hand, he helped the people around him because he loved doing it, not because it was his duty. He'd grown up poor on a farm in Southwest Michigan with an abusive father, and early on he vowed never to be like the man he'd seen hitting the farm horse on the forehead with a two-by-four. Instead, he took his mother, whom he did consider a saint for her kindness, her patience, and her prayers for her children, as his life model.

When we moved to Gallup, on the edge of the Navajo Nation, some of the members of my father's new congregation at Tohlakai suffered from alcohol addiction. My dad was deeply moved by how it affected not only the alcoholic but entire families, and he got a member of AA from Gallup to start evening meetings there. He saw fatherless children and took them fishing with my brothers, included them in hot dog roasts, and piled them into the pickup to go sledding. At my father's funeral, a grown man who had gone on these boyhood jaunts with our dad, talked about how much that had meant to him. Whereas I had left the church, this man was still an active member, maybe in part because of my father's kindness.

My father definitely preached to convert, however. At funerals, he preached that "the wages of sin is death," always hoping to save those standing around the grave from an eternity in hell. He picked up every hitchhiker he could. Countless times, I sat in the back seat and heard him launch into the same talk with his captive audience.

"Do you have sheep at home?" he would ask. This was invariably a gratuitous question, as Diné life centered on raising sheep.

"Yeah. Sure."

"I'm sure you take good care of your sheep—taking them out to graze and get water. You watch out for coyotes that might attack them. You put them in the corral at night. You would know if one of your sheep was missing, right?"

The hitchhiker would nod, probably already regretting having accepted the ride.

"And if a sheep was missing, you would leave the others in the corral and go out to look for the lost one?"

The hitchhiker nodded again.

"Jesus told a story about the Good Shepherd who goes after one lost sheep. He doesn't want even one sheep to die. The Bible calls Jesus the Good Shepherd because he doesn't want you and me to be lost, either. Anyone who believes in Jesus will go to heaven when they die. If we don't believe in him, the Bible says we will go to hell, where there is weeping and gnashing of teeth."

While he felt and showed concern for the lives of people in the here and now, his greatest concern was for their lives in the hereafter, and any way he could reach them for Christ was beneficial. He believed that traditional Diné ceremonies must be eradicated because they were of the Evil One. Some practices, like summer squaw dances (also called that by Diné, despite the otherwise pejorative term *squaw*) were mainly social but still wrong, in his mind. Other ceremonies were for healing. One in particular represented a form of what I see as restorative justice: the Enemy Way Ceremony, performed for returning soldiers to help relieve them of pre- and post-combat stress and return them to connections with family, community, and Native culture. To my dad and missionaries like him, all indigenous ceremonies had to go.

He saw rules that traditional Diné lived by as superstitious restrictions that fostered fear if they were broken. In his mind, Christianity could relieve people of those fears and offered the pathway to an afterlife in heaven. Diné friends have told me that many people have tremendous fear about breaking

Crevice 65

the taboos of traditional Diné ways. But fear of breaking cultural and religious rules is part of living socially; rules have, at least initially, existed to prevent behavior that can damage the group. Many restrictions in traditional Diné culture have to do with living in harmony with the natural world or have their origins in common sense, such as rules about water use in an arid land. As in many cultures, the origin of these rules has often been forgotten, so the proscriptions can seem irrational, not connected to real life any longer. The replacement religion and culture my father felt duty-bound to offer meant tearing apart a culture that had functioned well, but not perfectly—like any culture, my dad's included.

On one hand, Dad believed it was his mission to destroy the aspects of Diné culture that he saw as a false religion, and, on the other, paradoxically, he was passionately curious about the culture, even the parts of it that he believed must be wiped out. He was able to live within this contradiction because he saw Diné religion and culture as two separate things, which is not how traditional Diné experience them. To them, all of life and how we live it is one great, interconnected whole. I learned this from Diné elders and healers, not from Bilagáana missionaries.

I've never been more aware than I am at this point in the 21st century of the necessity for vetting information sources. And I have to say that my father's sources were often suspect—White missionaries with their soul-saving agenda, White traders with their commercial agenda, the federal government with its assimilation policies, and Diné who had embraced Christianity within the post-colonial ethos and would thus have a bias against their own traditions.

Sometime after my father's years of preaching were over, he, my brother Ed, and I went for a drive after a holiday dinner. We saw a man by the side of the road with his thumb out. Seeing the hitchhiker triggered a memory for my dad, who still had memories then, and he told us about recently picking up a Navajo man.

"He was a young man," my father said. "I asked him where he was from. He said Twin Lakes. I told him I used to hold Sunday night services there. 'Oh, you're a missionary,' he said. Then he asked me, 'Why did you missionaries ever come here? Why did you have to come and destroy our culture?' He was so bitter. So angry." Dad sounded bewildered. "I told him that wasn't true. We loved their culture."

Ed is much more able than I am to confront both of our parents with the flaws in their logic, and he does it lightly. He is a middle child, while I am the firstborn. Gently he said, "Really, Dad, you were. Destroying their culture." I was grateful to Ed for articulating what I thought but felt unable to say.

"No." That was all my father said, his voice laden with sorrowful protest. Not understanding. Maybe he even recognized a grain of truth in the young man's words or in what Ed said. He could not accept it.

Neither of my parents would have said that converting people to Christianity was also about converting them from traditional Diné ways to White ways of living. Within their missionary circle, few if any questioned whether or not those might be the same thing—Christian belief and mainstream culture in North America. It didn't occur to them that they were interlarding the majority way of life into their message, as if that were part and parcel of Christianity.

My mother's viewpoint was filled with her own pain, which so often caused her to be caustic. Her acceptance of the received missionary and government perspectives flowed through her demeaning speech and actions. The physician's first principle, "Do no harm," was also embedded in my mother's nursing practice, and she followed it, as so many other rules, to the letter. But she limited that code to providing physical medical help. She saw the effort to force Indigenous assimilation as a good thing, not harmful. And, generally, as Janice told me in the Girls' Room, she was not liked by people who saw deeper than her willingness to provide nursing care.

My father was a critical thinker, though always within the framework of a World War II veteran, a patriot, and a zealous evangelical Christian missionary. He was also, in many ways, a humanitarian, insofar as that did not conflict with his religious beliefs. As my mother's corrosiveness came from her early pain, my father's desire to help came from his pain as the son of a physically abusive father, whom he was determined not to emulate.

Curiosity is often a saving grace, and my father had it even after he began to lose his mental faculties. I, too, was curious about the Diné world that surrounded me. I wanted to learn to speak Diné bizaad. I ate the food, absorbed the love of the people I knew and loved them back. I embraced my parents' beliefs during childhood, but I sometimes secretly edged outside them. I relished my summer lullabies––the ceremonial drums and chanting that floated down from the hill above the mission. I would have liked to peer around a juniper tree when I heard them, to see what was happening, no matter how much I also believed my mother and father when they condemned the happenings.

From the stories I've told here, it's clear that, as a child, I observed and absorbed the differences in the ways my mother and father lived as guests in Navajo Country. Their ways often contrasted sharply, rising to the level of heated verbal conflict between them. Not until I reached high school did I begin to disagree with the beliefs they shared, even when they lived them out differently. It would be several more years before I understood the damage caused by how White missionaries drew a separation between religion and culture, thinking in all sincerity that they were offering a great gift. However, on an unconscious level, I was deciding where I stood. At first, as children often do, I aligned myself without knowing I was taking a stand.

I have a sharp memory from when I was four and hadn't lived in Dinétah for long. The house the mission board had assigned us in Shiprock stood on a hill overlooking the main road. The living room had a large picture window that looked directly onto Jack's Trading Post. We could watch people pull up in their horse-drawn wagons and go in bearing hand-woven rugs, bags of raw wool, or Bluebird flour bags wrapped around turquoise and silver jewelry. They came out with Bluebird sacks full of flour, red cans of coffee, bags of sugar, and boxes of canned goods. Old men sat along one exterior wall of the trading post visiting while their horses ate from their nosebags.

One day, we had visitors from Michigan, and they stood watching the scene unfold below. I was playing on the living room floor, when I heard one of them say, "Just look at those Indians down there."

By then I probably knew that Diné could be called *Indians*, but I heard something denigrating in the tone. Somewhat righteously, I imagine, and without a pause, I said, "They're not Indians. They're nice Navajos." I wasn't punished; I would remember it if I had been. But I was undoubtedly reprimanded for disrespecting an adult.

As an adolescent, I became conscious of wanting to truly belong to the people who surrounded me, to be one of them. There is a minor incident that stands large in my memory. Our high school choir was bused to Red Valley, Arizona, where our church had one of its missions. Before our performance, the Diné church ladies stood behind long tables to serve a traditional Diné meal of mutton stew and frybread. We lined up on the other side, and when I reached the tables, Mrs. Redhouse (Diné), the wife of the missionary there, greeted me by name. She handed me a bowl of stew, and I took the industrial sized salt shaker and shook a generous amount into my stew. Mrs. Redhouse laughed. "You're just like us. You love salt." A warm glow suffused my chest. I had been seen. Some Bilagáana students from the main mission stood near me, and I hoped they'd heard her. I wanted them to know who I belonged with. I had added all that salt because I knew that traditional foods were cooked without it. You were expected to add it later.

When the washing of diapers, the canning of fruits and vegetables, the cooking of gallons and gallons of soups and stews had been done, when there were no more church services to accompany, and most of all, when my father had more or less retired, my mother's harshness softened and diminished. My father preached whenever he was asked, until he fainted one Sunday on the podium. He continued to deliver Bibles to a stand at a Gallup truck stop, and he went regularly to the nursing home where he would spend his last years, so he could read the Bible in Diné bizaad to residents there.

In North America at large, in the Navajo Nation, and even in the evangelical mission world, an emergence from post-colonial policies and practices was in progress, and this seems to have had something of an effect on my mother. When she moved from my youngest brother's home into a nursing home, she was genuinely pleased to have a Diné roommate, a woman she already knew. Two days after Hilda's death, my mother had a stroke, and four days later she passed away. To me, this was not unlike a spouse dying within days of their partner. I chose to take my mother's departure so close to Hilda's as additional evidence that she had changed and grown with changing circumstances in the world around her.

I hesitate to write that my mother's prejudices can almost be seen as a gift because I am definitely not advocating or excusing her racism. But, if Janice was right, and I think she was, my mother's expressions of antipathy, even when only felt, not heard, could have given the Diné people who knew her, something to resist. It was probably unlikely that anyone would abandon their traditions because of her influence. Or maybe I'm projecting, and her attitudes eventually became something for me to confront.

My father's genuine interest in the people he met, on the other hand, made it more likely that they would readily trade in their traditional practices for Christianity along with its cultural trappings. It was my father's example I followed as a guest in Dinétah. In fact, perhaps how I related to life around me was one of my earliest steps away from both of them— taking my own path, which would turn out to be different from both of theirs. I didn't feel as if I was taking any sort of a stand. I was only doing what seemed natural.

Acculturation is generally defined as adaptation to a culture different from one's own, typically the dominant one. I acculturated in certain ways, not to the culture that prevailed in the US at the time, but to the one that surrounded me and dominated so much of my early life. No one exerted any pressure on me to assimilate, the way the US government and missionaries did on Indigenous people. I did so mostly unconsciously because Diné people surrounded me with love and acceptance, because I viewed what enfolded me as positive, desirable, and natural, whether in spite of or because of my parents' varying views and actions.

Recently my brother Rick interviewed a Diné woman on her thoughts about missionaries. She was a child in Teec Nos Pos when our family lived there and attended the mission school. She spoke of how missionaries entered Diné homes without a thought as to whether or not they were welcome or belonged there. "And we served you food. This wasn't reciprocated." And then she said, "But your family invited us into your home." Her voice took on a sound of surprise, almost amazement. She repeated it. "You had us into your home! And your mother served us cookies. She gave us medicine, probably from her own stash. We knew she was," and here she used the Diné phrase meaning, *the one who carries medicine.* She laughed, "She was a pharmacist. From her own stash."

 "From her own stash" was an incorrect but generous assumption. In reality, the hospital at Rehoboth provided my mother with various medicines she could distribute, including injectable penicillin. But the interview with Sharla helped me see my parents, and especially my mother, in a different light from what Janice had said to me in the Girls' Room. We all have public and private personae, and in this telling of how I saw my parents encounter and influence the lives of many Diné people, I have exposed what went on behind the scenes. Sometimes the private spilled over into the public enough that people saw my parents in contrast with each other, in the way that Janice had undoubtedly overheard from adults.

In a conversation with my mother, a few years before her death, I said something about her attitudes toward the Diné people. Her reply has left me still parsing the layers of its meaning. She said, "You and Dad always loved them so much. I felt like there wasn't any room for me to love them."

Crevice 74

PART II
SELF

Crevice 76

Border Town

I. HOMETOWN

Gallup. The town of legends. Nat King Cole immortalized it in "Get Your Kicks on Route 66." Bob Dylan famously lied that he was raised in Gallup, New Mexico in his first radio interview on the WNYC's *Folk Festival*. The town likes to call itself the "Indian Captital of the World" and has celebrated this putative status annually since 1921 by holding the Intertribal Indian Ceremonial, hosted by Indigenous performers and attended by visitors from around the world. But, in daily parlance, Gallup is more often known as "Drunktown," memorialized as such in the 2015 indie film, *Drunktown's Finest*.

More than half a century after our family first moved to Gallup, I moved back. People asked why, and their tone said, "Of all places!"

I told them, "It's my hometown." I've often called it that over the years. I write a column for the *Gallup Independent* four times a year and have had work published in the *Gallup Journey*. I've had four book signings in Gallup and been interviewed for a feature article in the town newspaper. I volunteered as a writer in residence in a fifth-grade classroom. Two of my seven brothers and my niece and her family live there, and my parents are buried there. Occasionally, I join family in Gallup for holidays or for the milestones we share. I've come back for the funerals of schoolmates and their family members.

I call Gallup my hometown, but I don't think of it as home. When I'm asked where I'm from, I say, "Teec Nos Pos." T'iis Názbas in Diné bizaad. But Teec Nos Pos is not home either; it became Home Not Home when we left it.

II. LEAVING THE CENTER

It was my fault we moved to Gallup in 1957, away from Teec Nos Pos, deep within the Navajo Nation, where my parents were missionaries. To this day, although Teec Nos Pos stands in the western half of the Nation, I think of it as the center. The beloved center. I was nine years old when our family moved, and it was because I had been deathly homesick at the mission boarding school. On my first visit home, I had pleaded with my mother and father not to send me back.

"You wanted to go," they said. But I hadn't known what boarding school was. "You have to live with your choice," they said to my eight-year-old self. In the end, they decided it wasn't working, but they made me finish out the school year.

On the day we left Teec Nos Pos for Gallup, a long orange moving van pulled up in front of the adobe missionary house. At the very end, our bicycles were tied to the back of the truck, and the truck churned through dust, headed for Gallup. In the way of flashfloods, dark clouds suddenly filled the sky. Rain began to pelt down as we piled into the station wagon. Water cascaded from the sky, and the arroyo across from the mission filled to the brim, muddy brown water raging down toward the trading post.

It was a flood of mythical proportion, and one of the boys took it as a sign. "Maybe we're not supposed to leave," he said.

I'd been thinking it and said, "Yeah. Let's stay."

My mother turned and looked at me. "You'd have to go back to boarding school."

My stomach dropped, and I was silent.

III. BACK AND BACK AGAIN

Recently, I interviewed a White woman for a writing project. She was consulting on health initiatives in Gallup at the time. "I don't know how much a part of your life Gallup is anymore," she said.

"Always." I said without hesitating.

She laughed, and I smiled. This border town has had a hold on me since I was nine years old, and it probably will as long as I am in my right mind. Gallup is called a *border town* because it stands on an edge of the largest Indigenous nation in the United States, the Navajo Nation. It is a magnet that both attracts and repels me.

When I'm away from Gallup and see images of the town in the media, I immediately place them in my personal geography. I keep up with current events. I applaud changes for the better and feel bitter sorrow over things that need to change and don't. Over the years, I have considered moving back to Gallup more than once.

In fact, I have left and moved back several times. The first leave-taking was outside my control. It happened in 1959, when my only sister was hospitalized at NIH with leukemia, and our family moved to Maryland to be with her. In 1961, we returned to Gallup where I finished high school and then left a second time, this time for college. I came back summers to work at Dandee Supermarket. I'd worked there during high school, too, for $1.25 an hour and a measure of sanity—a world away from the mission school. I returned again in the early 1970s to teach, leaving a year and a half later. Back again in

1981 after a life-shattering divorce to live for a few months with my brother's family.

And, once again in 2018, something drew me back—back to Drunktown. Back to this border town.

IV. A DIFFERENT GEOGRAPHY
The town sprawls amid once coal-rich hills, a hundred thirty miles from Teec Nos Pos. We had been there only a few times before we moved. It was one thing to drive through, stopping to wait for a passing train or for my parents to do some grocery shopping while we sat in the car for what seemed like hours. It was culture shock to begin living there:

> The soft, cream-colored arroyo bottom turns
> > into asphalt streets.
> Round hogans are rendered into squares
> > topped by triangles.
> Horses and wagons rolling slow in Native time
> > transform into pickups,
> > whipping around corners—
> > sudden danger.
> Bright blue air traded for a gritty shroud—
> > twenty-six defunct mining towns still
> > spread their dust.
> Drumbeats and summer chants from the hill
> > switch to shrill
> > klaxons of rattling freight trains.
> The great golden rock pile becomes hills
> > peppered with stores, churches, bars.
> Gone from the center.
> > Shifted to an edge.

We moved into the yellow brick house at 213 West Green. Here, houses stood close together. Our neighbors were all Bilagáana except for one Japanese family. No Diné lived alongside us anymore. I began

Crevice 80

to learn, little by little, what a border town was. It has taken me a lifetime to make meaning of it.

V. BORDER TOWN

The main border towns are these: Gallup, the most well-known, except maybe Winslow, Arizona because of the Eagles song; there is also Farmington, New Mexico; Cortez in southern Colorado; and Flagstaff and Holbrook, both in Arizona.

These towns both serve and exploit the people of the Nation, the Diné. They supply goods similar to those provided by trading posts in the Nation. They provide commodities that people can't or don't grow or produce and sell larger items like cars and trucks, appliances, electronics, and mobile homes. Border town businesses exploit Native people by selling these goods, especially durable ones, at inflated prices with exorbitant interest rates. In return, businesses pay low prices for fine jewelry and rugs crafted by Diné, Zuni, and Hopi and resell them to tourists at huge profits. Without Indigenous people, tourism in Gallup would be limited to an overnight stay en route to natural wonders like the Grand Canyon or Monument Valley.

VI. WHY INDEED

People asked why when I said I was moving back to Gallup in 2018. Again. Really, I moved to an edge between edges, to land a few short miles north of town. Gallup and other border towns were built for commerce and religion. They are not lovely. But all around them lies beauty of heartbreaking wonder.

I came back
> To hear the wind rise suddenly, soughing
>> through piñon and juniper.
> For the hills.
> The mesas.

I came
> For the flat chocolate slabs of sitting-rocks,
>> from there to watch the glory
>> of dusk—the pink flush, gold blaze,
>> the ginger and orange, the scarlet—
>> all diminishing to mauve and indigo.

I came
> For the smell of rain-washed earth and sage.
> For cedar smoke at night.
> To cut small sprays of scarlet paintbrush
> and purple asters,
> to line them with juniper,
> place them in a small brown vase.

I came
> To hear Diné spoken every day.
> To speak Diné with others.
> Perhaps to finish something I'd begun.
> To make the circle round.
>> Maybe that.

VII. CULTURE SHOCK

When we first moved into Gallup, the way I saw Diné people became the greatest shock. I wandered downtown for a cherry coke at the Rexall drugstore or to the library and came face to face with Diné stumbling toward me. Their eyes were red and swollen, weeping, their clothes dirty and torn. When they came close enough, I smelled the sickening sweet stench of alcohol. Sometimes instead of bumbling toward me, they lay in a huddle next to a building, sleeping or blubbering.

When I got home I told my mother, "I'm scared of them."

She said, "You don't need to be scared. If they're drunk, you can knock them over with your little finger." I didn't believe it for a second, but I learned to steel myself and keep walking when a drunk passed me or tried to talk to me.

In Teec Nos Pos, people walked upright. The women wore traditional satin and velvet with loads of turquoise-and-silver jewelry. They tended their flocks and fields of corn and melons, took their sheep up the mountain in summer for good grazing. They rolled up to the mission in wooden wagons to fill fifty-gallon barrels with water and gave us rides to the trading post. They brought loads of wool to the trading post to be packed into burlap bags as tall as a man and walked out with coffee and sugar and Bluebird flour.

Close by the border town, Diné women wore long, gathered cotton skirts and button-down cotton blouses, less jewelry. They owned sheep, but not as many. If they drove, it was pickups, not horses and wagons. Homes were tarpaper-covered rectangles, not round, earthen hogans. I saw poverty, but I didn't understand that it was because the original, sustainable way of life was mostly gone, and nothing had replaced it. Alcoholism was evident on the land skirting Gallup, as if the town had slowly leaked into the border and beyond.

VIII. THE NATURE OF BORDERS
The border that cannot be permeated doesn't exist.
> I know a man,
>> carried on his father's shoulders
>> when he was a baby,
>> held above the water of the
>> sewers of Berlin,
>> crossing the wall from East to West.

Crevice 83

Cell walls are semi-permeable membranes.
    Our lives depend on the exchange of
    nutrients, oxygen, inorganic ions,
    waste products, and water
    across those thin barriers.

My colleague comes up too close;
    I step back.
    I excuse myself,
    saying my trifocals make
    it uncomfortable to stand so close.
    But really, our personal boundaries
    are not the same.

I tell my Hispanic students,
    children of undocumented immigrants,
    about marrying my
    New Zealand friend, so we could
    get permission to stay in each other's
        countries.
    "Isn't that illegal?" one of them asks.
    "Yes," I say, "but I don't believe in
        borders.
    We should be able to cross
    over into any country we want."
    They are silent.
    No one has said this to them before.

Poland could be said to have
    too many borders.
    It has been taken,
    retaken,
    gained independence,
    only to be taken again.
    And again.

New Mexico, the state in which
    I have lived most of my life,

was taken from Mexico,
along with parts of California,
Arizona,
Texas,
following the border war
known in the US as the Mexican War,
known in Mexico as
the American Intervention in Mexico.

Borders are In Between places. They are places where contact and contrasts take place. They are places where we rub up against each other and discover differences in language, customs, religions, and life goals. In *Gone Native in Polynesia*, Ian Campbell writes that cultural contact is simply "an abstraction of what happens when people from different societies meet and attempt to satisfy their respective needs." This is a benign view of what happens in the borderlands. But Campbell goes on to add a critical piece, saying which group makes the most cultural adjustments "depends on how important the transaction is to the respective parties, location (on whose territory is the transaction taking place), or which party has the most coercive power." And therein lies the recipe for the conflict that so often happens at borders.

Some boundaries, such as cell membranes, are natural, and, unless a disruptive process such as disease occurs, exchanges pass freely across them, to the benefit of all. But the borders we humans create are arbitrary. Because of their artificial nature, when a crossing is attempted without permission, conflict occurs. The ancestral lands of the Indigenous Tohono O'odham Nation, stretch from southern Arizona in the US into the Mexican state of Sonora. To them the Mexico-US border is eminently artificial. Originally, crossing of boundaries did not exist; there were only homelands.

One of my brothers has lived most of his adult life in Gallup. He says of the conflict that exists here, "I've learned to be comfortable with being uncomfortable." Discomfort arises because he lives in the imaginary space that lies between the White and Diné worlds. There is confusion as to where and whether he belongs. It is in the nature of borderlands—this not knowing.

IX. CHANGED AND UNCHANGING
Nighttime, the second Saturday in November, and downtown Gallup is teeming with people in winter coats, scarves, and stocking caps. It is the night of the monthly Arts Crawl. Galleries and shops are lit, doors open. Outdoor vendors sell crafts, coffee, and snacks. The air crackles with good will. Businesses that were once grimy and tired have gotten facelifts, making their facades clean and appealing.

I enter a Diné-owned shop where every piece is thoughtfully and lovingly curated. An outsized painting shows four Yé'ii. Holy People. In a traditional painting, the Yé'ii would be stylized, painted with squared lines, offering no sense of the men beneath the masks. This one is full of mystery, humor and humanness, revealing the emotions and character of the subjects and the artist. Shelves in the store contain sleek marble sculptures, fabric arts that blend traditional craft with contemporary motifs. Black-and-white photos that showcase the high desert.

I leave the bustle and noise of Coal Avenue to see what, if anything, is happening on Route 66. On the way, I pass a puddled, unlit alley where the backs of those refurbished fronts reveal dark, rough-hewn stone. The bleak, narrow passage is emblematic of borders, boundaries that still exist, unchanged.

Gallup—the same, yet different; changed and unchanging.

Earlier that week, I saw three small Indigenous boys leaning against a low adobe wall in a middle-class neighborhood. They watched two black-and-whites pull up to join a parked paddy wagon. White officers stepped out and joined a Native policeman, the driver of the wagon. I asked myself, Why all the firepower? The Diné officer had already cuffed a Native man who sat on the ground, head bowed. I wondered what the boys were thinking—if they were simply curious, if they saw the unfolding scene as an exciting crime drama, or if they felt ashamed, living in this town where Natives have been unwanted for so long. Except for the money they bring.

X. CONFLICT

I was twelve the summer our family camped in a tiny trailer fifteen miles outside Gallup in Tohlakai. The little green shelter was parked by the chapel where my father was the missionary. The Goldtooths lived a few hundred yards from us. Mr. Goldtooth was one of several people who might show up on a Sunday morning red-eyed, smelling of booze and still under the influence from a twenty-four-hour bender in town. His usual self-control destroyed by drink, he would shout out in the middle of a sermon or prayer. Ours was not a shouting church, so it was noticeable. The yelling ended in loud, histrionic crying. The services went on as if nothing unusual were happening. I knew Mr. Goldtooth hadn't always been that way. He had helped build the chapel on his family's land and had worked as a missionary's interpreter, years earlier.

One night that summer, I got to feel up close how the clash between the border town and Dinétah had seeped across the line into Tohlakai. Our family had finished supper when Birdie Goldtooth came to the trailer. At first, I thought she just wanted to hang out, but then I saw in her eyes that something was wrong.

"My dad's drunk again," she said. "He's really mad. He's yelling and tearing up the house."

My mother heard her. "Why don't you and your sisters come over and sleep in the chapel?" she suggested.

They brought their bedrolls, and I begged to join them. We laid our pallets out on the floor, and the problem of the evening turned into a sleepover. We chattered and giggled until a fist pounded on the door, silencing us. It was Mr. Goldtooth. He yelled at us to open the door. "This is my chapel. I built it. Open the door!"

I tensed. Mr. Goldtooth rattled the door and pounded some more. I was petrified it would come crashing down.

The girls didn't seem fazed, now that we were safely locked in. By silent agreement, we said nothing, and he left after what seemed like an hour, though it was probably only minutes. As I lay there, letting my body go soft again, it came to me that being safe was unusual for my friends while being terrified was unusual for me.

XI. EDGE EFFECTS
At the Scandinavian Yoga and Meditation School, I was assigned to weed and thin a large field of young parsnips. I noticed that whenever I came to an edge of the field, the parsnips were much smaller and thinner, scrawny really, than those a few rows in. They bore the effects of the wind, the cold, dust from passing cars, and maybe other stresses I knew nothing about.

Ecologists and mappers refer to *edge effects*, particularly where ecosystems overlap. In those places flora and fauna compete for resources, and the competition can result in peaking or falling biodiversity. For example, where the eastern escarpment of the Andes meets the tropics in Ecuador, a remarkable diversity of bird species lives. Birds find what the mountains have and have not, and all that the jungle has and has not, which creates an environment amenable to diversity but one that also fosters conflict and competition.

Other things happen on ecological edges, too; invasive species exploit the vulnerability of edges. Plants, such as my parsnips, struggle to thrive on the edges. When I was tending the parsnips, I thought of the puny roots as offering a buffer for the vegetables at the center—bearing all the exigencies that occur in the borders. I drew an analogy to people who live on the margins—how we may also provide a cushion for those who live at the center. Maybe there is always conflict, discomfort, in the edge places, in border towns—for everyone—whether Brown or White. Some people thrive on the discomfort, find their creativity and growth challenged and become productive, venture farther out. Others bear the brunt of the stresses that come to bear on them at the verge and perhaps retreat toward the center or withdraw into the numbness of addiction. Still others experience the edge and ponder what goes on there.

XII. LOVE/HATE
I love Gallup, and I hate it; my Diné friends testify to this even more than I. When I was young, I didn't know how my Navajo friends felt about Gallup. A Diné woman recently told me, "Natives won't tell you what they really think. They'll tell you what they think you want to hear." I was hurt, and I had a hard time

believing it. But it's possible I only get the truth when Diné feel they're talking to each other, and I'm just an invisible observer.

My friend Alice Whitegoat laughs as she tells me about being a teenager in Gallup, sneaking down into the Rio Puerco with her friends on a summer night, about the tattletale who didn't know how to have fun, a Presbyterian convert. And then she shows me the black-and-white photo where she is marching at the front of the protest after the Gallup police shot and killed Larry Casuse. The police had their photo taken, posed over his body as if he were a deer they'd bagged. Three hundred students walked out of Gallup High School the day of Larry's funeral. We never knew the truth of what happened when he was slain—what really went down. Larry had remonstrated hard at the State House in Santa Fe against police brutality and the exploitation of Natives by the Gallup liquor industry. Not until after his tragic death were the state alcohol licensing laws changed.

The summer after Larry Casuse was killed, I went back to UNM to take courses toward my master's degree. One class required a local field study, and I called my project "Gallup: An Ugly City." On a south-side hill, I took images of sprawling ranch-style homes with landscaped front yards—the homes of those who profited from liquor sales and from selling the work of Native hands to tourists. I photographed bars and pawnshops. I went to the north side to take images of the condemned hovels in which people still lived.

When I presented my report, a student took exception to my title. "Those houses on the hill," she said, "they're not ugly."

I had already called attention to the fact that those houses were built on exploitation. I reiterated, "The people who own those houses gained their money from alcohol sales to Natives, from price gouging, and unfair lending practices."

Crevice 90

The instructor understood and reinforced my argument, but the woman, a public school educator said, "Still..."

I shook my head.

Gallup. Border town. The place In Between that oozes over its borders. Gallup. My hometown. The place I keep coming back to. The place I love and hate.

XIII. AT THE ROOT

I hadn't seen alcoholism in Teec Nos Pos. In Gallup, I heard White grownups speculate that Natives were genetically predisposed to alcoholism. According to the former Director of Substance Abuse Treatment and Prevention for the Navajo Nation, a medical doctor, research does not support the theory of genetic predisposition. In fact, the demographics say there is no higher incidence of alcoholism among the Diné than among any other group of people.

The question then arises: Why does it appear otherwise? One reason is that the Navajo and Zuni Nations, the reservations closest to Gallup, are dry by law. If people want to drink, they must go to a border town or a bar just off the reservation to do so. It is also forbidden to bring alcohol, even in closed containers, into the Nation. This makes Diné who want to drink highly visible in the border towns.

There are root causes for addiction. In this case, colonization in its manifold manifestations destroyed a way of life that functioned well—the way of life that was still largely in existence in Teec Nos Pos in the 1950s. Near border towns, the story was otherwise. The colonial system did not replace that effective subsistence economy with a viable alternative. Colonization has brought with it poverty and often purposelessness to Indigenous peoples the world over.

In Dinétah, excess drinking numbs the generational pain of trauma and loss—loss of homeland, family, language, and culture. Generations of Native people have been ripped from home and family and forcibly taken to boarding schools where the stated goal was to "make them White," to "pacify" them, "to kill the Indian but save the man."

XIV. MY PLACE IN THE BORDERLANDS
Sometimes, as on a sheet of stationery, a border serves as the edge; no stationery exists beyond it. More often, a border lies between two places. Sometimes, as with a living cell, the borderline is microscopically thin. Other times there is a space that is much wider than a line, a sort of no-man's-land. When I first came to live in the Navajo Nation, I began a lifelong fall into a crevice between two worlds—into an invisible, yet very real, border. At first, I lived physically close to the center of the Nation. As a child, I thought I belonged there because that was my life. Then we moved to the border town, and I began to know that I had not belonged at the center, after all.

Maybe that is why I have kept coming back to Gallup. Because my place is here. In the borderland. The In Between place. Prickly and uncomfortable and rough-edged, full of conflict. We live here together, work here, make our art here. A place where no one quite belongs.

Naturalization

"Naturalization: becoming established **as if** native"
~ *Webster's Collegiate Dictionary*, Eleventh Edition
[Emphasis mine]

It would have made sense for me to feel angry or, at the very least, annoyed. Instead, my stomach flipped, and my throat tightened. The anxiety was momentary, but it had made itself known. The rest of my class had gotten there on time, and I had given them the day's assignment. Now I had to give it all over again for one student. One chronically late student. Tineesha. She found an empty desk, nonchalantly pulled off her puffy pink nylon jacket and deposited her book bag on the floor. Then she looked expectantly toward my desk.

With two fingers, I motioned for her to come up, gave her the handout, explained the assignment, and asked her to join one of the smaller critique groups. "Oh, I haven't finished my essay yet," she said.

I swallowed past the constriction again and said, "Why don't you go ahead and join a group anyway? You can give the others feedback. Part of your grade is based on you giving feedback. And maybe they can help you move forward with your essay, give you some suggestions."

"Actually, I didn't start it yet. Oh, except for that free-write we did in class last time."

Crevice 93

"Okay. Well then, you can decide how to best use your time, whether to draft your essay or give feedback. If you don't give feedback, though, you will lose some points, so you might want to draft later. Plus, your group may have some good ideas for you. And remember, the essay still has to be turned in on time." Tineesha nodded and went back to the desk where she'd left her jacket, took out her notebook and a pen and began writing.

I circulated among the groups, listening to their comments, making a few suggestions, recording points for peer feedback. When class was over, I went up to my office in the English Department. I stared out the window at the skeletal trees and gray sky. As I pondered my earlier reaction to Tineesha's work habits, storm clouds gathered on the horizon. Tineesha's way of doing Freshman Composition represented the extreme in my class, but the other two African American students were also more often late and asked more frequently for extensions on assignments than anyone else did.

As I watched the steely clouds roll in, however, I was less preoccupied with my students than with my feelings about their performance. Something shriveled inside me when I saw them appear to sabotage their success. My first inclination was to examine myself for racism, but it didn't take long for my thoughts to shift to Neale and the world I came to know intimately through her.

My naturalization process had begun at the door of a motel on Old Route 66 in Albuquerque, New Mexico, thirty years earlier. Neale and I were friends then, but it wouldn't be long before we became lovers. We'd gone to Albuquerque for the weekend, and around midnight, after seeing a late movie, we decided it was time to look for a place to stay. Old 66 is lined with one-story, courtyard-style motels from the Mother Road's heyday. Today, the seamy side of life—prostitution, drug deals and transient stopovers—takes place in them. But in 1973, while tourists stayed in multi-storied chain establishments just off the new Interstate, we New Mexicans found comfortable, cheap lodging in the old, low-slung motels there.

The vacancy sign at our first pick was still lit that night, but the office was dark, so we rang the buzzer. A frowsy, middle-aged White woman came to the door in her housecoat and looked us up and down and back and forth, when we said we wanted a room. I'm a medium-height White woman, in my early twenties then. Neale is Black, almost six-foot-four with her Afro, my age. She was solidly built but not fat; in the dark she could easily have been mistaken for a man.

"We're full," the woman said abruptly.

"But the sign..." I said.

"I forgot to turn it out."

"Come on," Neale said. "We'll go someplace else." Back in the car, her voice turned hot. She said, "It's because I'm Black. They had rooms."

"But she said she forgot..."

"She didn't forget. They don't forget to turn out the sign when leaving it on is going to get them out of bed in the middle of the night. You go to the window alone at the next place, and I guarantee we'll get in."

She was right. After that, whenever we needed a motel, I went to the window, and we were never again turned away. That experience on Old 66 was like a needle shoved under my skin, inoculating me with a sample of the disease, creating the antibodies that would make me see things through Neale's eyes, sometimes even experience them the same way, the way generations of her family had.

As we became family, Neale tutored me in a new language. *Nappy hair* was too curly, unkempt. Of interest is the fact that this meaning of *nappy* does

Crevice 95

not appear in *Webster's Eleventh Edition Collegiate Dictionary*, although the British variant, meaning *diaper*, does. Now, at the opening of the twenty-first century, despite its absence from the dictionary, *nappy* is a word that many Whites are familiar with from movies and television; in the early seventies, learning this and other words was part of my naturalization. *Good hair* in African American English is hair that's not so curly—the less curly, the better. A *conk* is what a man gets when he wants straight hair. *Ashy* skin is just dry skin, but on a Black person it's gray, ashy looking. An *Oreo* is a black person who's Black on the outside, White on the inside, lacking in self-pride. *High yellow* refers to someone whose skin is very light.

CP time means *Colored People's time*, and it's not much different from what I grew up with in Dinétah—*Indian Time*. It's a kind of time that flows with the larger rhythms of life—the seasons, the tides, the changing from sun to moon, rather than with the sweep of a second hand. When people are attending to these bigger increments of time, there is no such thing as being a few minutes or even a few hours late. I never internalized Indian Time. My mother shouted at us every day except Saturday as she propelled us toward the door on our way to church or school, "Would it kill you to be a few minutes early for a change?" That's what I internalized, and it's helped me fit into the world of clocks and day planners with ease. So much was against Neale's and my partnership that it was fortunate for me and for the relationship that she didn't operate on CP time any more than I did.

In my university office, rain began slapping the windows, and the dark tree limbs swayed like small twigs about to break. I figured Tineesha was operating on CP time, and I thought of other possible reasons for her actions. She's a freshman, I thought, maybe overwhelmed by being away from home and being on a large university campus with all that entails. She could be afraid of success. Maybe she just hasn't learned yet how to prioritize—not unusual in freshmen.

But what about me? I didn't have to dig very deep to know that my anxiety came from wanting my Black students to do well, to not be laid bare to any criticism from their White peers. I didn't want anyone to be able to lump them into a stereotype, and I knew stereotypes abounded. I wanted success for them, but I didn't know if there was anything I could or should be doing differently to help them achieve it. And I was painfully aware of my own Whiteness.

Neale had opened to me a treasure of African-American literature—Countee Cullen, Lucille Clifton, Maya Angelou, and Toni Morrison. We read aloud to each other, nights and Saturday mornings, propped against our twin reading pillows, and also on road trips. I remember exactly when and where we read Alice Walker's *Meridian*. We were driving to San Antonio, Texas, to visit friends for Thanksgiving. Somewhere between Artesia and Carlsbad, under a fine autumn rain, my voice broke, and I couldn't read more for grief. I don't remember now specifically what I was grieving. It could have been the troubled relationship between Meridian and her mother, the relationship that made Meridian feel she needed to ask forgiveness because she existed—not unlike my relationship with my mother. It could have been for the way we humans in our deepest intimacies are capable of such hurtfulness. It could have been for shame and hopelessness over the way race has become an excuse for not extending ourselves in love.

Whatever it was, Neale pulled our sky-blue Beetle onto the desert shoulder and held me while I sobbed.

In New Mexico, Blacks represented less than two percent of the population in the seventies. "Just because we're only two percent of the population doesn't mean we're not here," Neale complained. "They need to stop calling New Mexico the tri-cultural state. Native American and Hispanic, yes. But there's no such thing as a White culture. There are Dutch and Italian, German and Polish cultures, but not White culture. And just because the Black presence is small, doesn't mean we haven't been here contributing. We've been in New Mexico since before the Civil War as cowboys and during and after the war as soldiers."

The size of the Black population meant we spent hours searching for Black hair products, and we were jubilant when we finally located a store on South Broadway in Albuquerque that stocked them. We searched until we found a Black barber in the same neighborhood to trim Neale's Afro after a Gallup beautician and I had both made her look less than presentable. I asked the barber if he knew how to cut White hair. "Of course," he said. "That's all I learned in barber school. I had to teach myself how to cut Black hair."

I found out that's how a lot of things are, how Black people, raised in the dominant culture, know so much more about White people than Whites do about Blacks. I saw that it wasn't very different from growing up lesbian in a straight world. Raised to be straight, I knew more about what it meant to be heterosexual than about who I might be in a gay world I had known nothing about for the longest time.

I experienced the odd effect of living in photonegative when we visited Neale's family in Brooklyn. At home in New Mexico, I sometimes felt that I lived in Neale's shadow. People who forgot my name always remembered hers. They remembered things she'd said; next to her I often felt small and, well, colorless. Intellectually sharp, a voracious reader, charming and outspoken, she was a presence to be reckoned with in any setting. It wasn't until we visited Brooklyn for the second time that I realized context had something to do with how memorable each of us was to the people who met us.

We were upstairs in Neale's sisters' bedroom, dressing to go out. "You know what?" I said, amazement in my voice. "Those people who came to the party this afternoon, they all remembered my name from when we were here last Christmas. They remembered things about me from our last visit. I couldn't believe it. Usually, it's you that people remember."

"That's because in New Mexico, I'm the one who's different. Here you're the one who's different. That's all. It's not that I'm more memorable. I keep telling you that."

Our early educations also showed up in silver and black. In the public schools of urban New York with their high Black enrollments, Neale had never once had an African American teacher. My first teachers, on the other hand, were all Black. Growing up in Teec Nos Pos, deep in the heart of Dinétah, my first school, which ran from kindergarten through second grade, was run by the Bureau of Indian Affairs (BIA). In the early fifties the federal government was one of few equal opportunity employers, so most teachers in the BIA schools were Black and came from places like Arkansas, Mississippi and Georgia to pass on the soft, round English of the Black South to Native American children who were just learning the language.

My first crush was on my younger brother's caramel-colored teacher who wore lipstick and smelled like perfume. I was looking for the mothering that my own mother seemed too busy with her five other children to give, and Miss Huff patiently listened to me chatter every afternoon after school, even letting me visit her tiny round-ended trailer while she cooked supper. Before I fell asleep at night, I imagined burying my face in the nubbly roughness of her knitted, ribbed beige dress and breathing in her smell while she cupped the back of my head in her hands.

I can only imagine that in the evening, when they spent time together, the teachers used words like the ones Neale would teach me—among them, *nappy* and *high yellow*. But in public, which consisted of the school, our family, and the traders' families, they lived the assimilated lives of professionals. They called themselves *colored* and were more refined by middle class, White standards than my mother was.

Of the two of us, Neale would undoubtedly have benefited more from having African American teachers, from seeing women whose careers might tell her, "I did it, and you can, too." Although they taught me nothing of African American culture and never spoke in front of me about the racism they'd experienced, though they appeared to be part of whatever I knew of mainstream culture, they might well have related differently with Neale and other Black children. Nevertheless, I benefited from these teachers in some different ways than Neale would have.

One day when I was in second grade, we were called out of the classroom, one by one, to a room that looked like a little clinic. I had never been in there before, so I looked around with interest at the examining table, the scale, the jars of cotton balls, tongue depressors, applicators, and medicines. A chart with rows of the capital letter E hung on one wall. The Es were placed upside down, backwards and sideways, and as they moved down the page, the letters got smaller and smaller.

Miss Huff was already in the room, sitting at a desk with a clipboard and pen. She told me to cover one eye with my hand and use the other hand to show the positions of the letter E. I moved my hand up and down and sideways with ease, sure that I was doing a fine job. The teacher-principal, Miss Holbrook, also Black, came in before I'd finished and stood beside Miss Huff. By this time, I had covered my other eye and was confidently showing the positions of the Es with my other hand. Miss Holbrook whispered loudly to Miss Huff, "Look at those hands, so white and skinny, compared to the brown chubby ones."

As soon as she said it, my stomach knotted up, and my fingers turned cold. I wanted to hide my face, and, in a way I did, by not showing that I had heard. I finished all the rows, but my feeling of accomplishment had vanished. Back in the classroom, I held my fingers below the top of my desk and stared at them. I knew there was something wrong with them, something wrong with me, and it was about the color of my skin.

I was one of three White children attending the school, and all the personnel were either Diné or African American. Ever since we'd moved to Navajo Country for my parents to take up missionary work when I was three, although I was racially part of the American majority, I almost always found myself in the minority. It was something I was accustomed to, and now I would say that being in the minority from day to day enriched my life. Even Miss Holbrook's words, while painful to hear, enriched me, helping me later to empathize more deeply than I otherwise might have with anyone who suffered discrimination. Those early experiences were like an alcohol swab, preparing my skin for that first needle prick on Old 66.

True naturalization takes place over time, through the mundane, through the breaking of bread, through experiences that enter one's consciousness slowly, often in such small increments that the events are scarcely noticed or recognized as bringing about deep transformation. Neale and I brought our family

Crevice 101

recipes to our kitchen, but it was when I ate with her family that I noticed some of the differences in how our families cooked. Her West Indian grandmother made turkey for Christmas dinner, but the gravy had a tomato base, and golden rings of onions floated in it, instead of the giblets in brown sauce that my mother made. Neale's stepfather, in a very big production, made peas and rice with pigtails, and I was amazed to see how long a pig's tail really is—more than a foot. Back at home I learned to cook collard greens in pot likker until the tastes of ham and brown sugar and greens had married into an irresistible mix of flavors and textures. I replicated Grandma's gravy when I roasted a chicken. I did not think that I was drawing sustenance from another culture and becoming part of it at its edges; some habits changed without Neale or me or anyone else taking notice.

I knew I had truly arrived in my adopted homeland when Neale said laughingly, sounding surprised at herself, "I almost called you *niggah* just now. You know, in the way only we can call each other that." A couple of days later, it happened; in a moment of hilarity, she called me the word I always referred to as the *N-word*. Maybe she couldn't do it without first preparing me. So I would know it was a good thing, a sign of belonging.

Often the things that knit us most tightly together are less the joys and more the difficulties we survive together. It makes some sense then, that I mark the beginning of my naturalization process at that motel on Old 66, with Neale's and my shared humiliation and anger. Much later, when Neale was trying to get into medical school, she paid a visit to the dean at the University of New Mexico School of Medicine. Afterwards, my hopes for her took a slide when she came home with a grim face. I poured tea and held her hand at the kitchen table.

"The woman barely even let me say anything. She took one look at me and said, 'We already have one of you. Why don't you try the law school?'"

Perhaps the greatest agent of naturalization comes from deep bonding experiences brought on by shared tragedy. One morning when we were getting ready for work, the phone rang. It was Neale's mother, calling from Brooklyn. She told Neale that her stepfather had died the night before of a heart attack. We decided we couldn't afford two plane tickets, so we made flight arrangements, and I drove Neale to the airport. When I got home that evening, she called. She sounded almost as if she were choking as she told me that Harold hadn't had a heart attack. A family member had stabbed him.

"How long did my mother think it would take me to find out what really happened? It's crazy here." Neale's voice broke.

"I'm coming there," I said.

Neale protested for about a second, then sounded relieved.

I arrived in Newark at noon the next day. Neale was right. It was pretty crazy, and I dove into the craziness, trying to help, to be a support. The party where everyone remembered me was really Harold's wake. Some of the guests continued to go along with the pretense that he had died of a heart attack. That was crazy in itself because Harold was a retired police officer, and of course his police brothers knew all the details.

I helped to serve the food people brought—hams, turkeys, casseroles, sweet potato and bean pies. I visited with the people who remembered me. I sat with the family at the High Episcopal funeral service and watched the police honor guard bear the casket out to the hearse. Afterwards we drove for miles and miles through glorious red, yellow, and rust foliage to the cemetery in Long Island. And for days we ate leftover black-eyed peas and collard greens and turkey.

Upstairs in my office, I couldn't help thinking about what Neale had missed out on by not having Black teachers. I speculated about the difference it could make for Tineesha and my other African American students to have a Black professor, someone who might be able to provide a better context for holding them accountable, someone who might more ably inspire them.

It was my practice to hold conferences with my students prior to the final revisions of their essays. Before our conference on the personal essay in progress, I'd read Tineesha's draft with pleasure. Her topic, a night of cruising the streets of Detroit, contained some vivid descriptions, but it seemed to need more action. I did my best to convey to her how strong I thought it already was. I made a few suggestions about where she might be able to give it more punch. When I got the final draft, I was disappointed to see that Tineesha had cleaned up some grammar and punctuation, but that she hadn't used any of the suggestions. I accepted that it was her story; I also knew that her previous experience with writing instruction, as with many college students, might have emphasized editing for conventions with little attention to making larger changes. Nevertheless, I felt I'd somehow failed her.

As we neared the end of the semester, it was clear that a few students could possibly fail the course. Not surprisingly, one of them was Tineesha. That spring, our entire town had embarked on its annual Reading Together Project. The selection was *The Color of Water: A Black Man's Tribute to His White Mother* by James McBride. In March, a month before the end of the semester, there would be discussion groups on campus and events in the community, including a free jazz saxophone concert by the author. I had read the book and been deeply moved by it. I decided to offer anyone who wanted to improve their grade extra credit for reading the book, attending one of the events and writing their impressions of both. I made sure that students who were in danger of failing were aware of their status and encouraged them to take advantage of the opportunity. No one did.

I think I'd hoped that the fact that James McBride is African American would make him accessible to a student like Tineesha. When I read the book a second time years later, I realized that it might be of more interest to someone struggling with identity issues related to mixed heritage, which didn't appear to fit Tineesha's situation. Nevertheless, it could have been enriching, part of what education is about.

In the end, all of my students but Tineesha managed to pull their grades up to passing. It pained me to give her the only failing grade in my class. And, in the end, I was left with questions, not so much about whether I'd done all I could, whether I'd failed this student, and whether my Whiteness had contributed to my failure. I was really more interested in myself and why I felt so strongly that I wanted this student to succeed and not only to succeed but to shine before the others in the class.

You think when you walk together through the everyday hardships and through tragedy, and you come out on the other side, that being family, belonging to each other, will never end. Neale's and my relationship did end after seven years, for a lot of reasons. Every intimate encounter transforms, some more than others. When the encounter is over, many of the changes that have taken place remain. Over time their edges become rounded, and they are, perhaps, less visible, but they are there.

Neale expanded my world in so many ways through literature, music, and intimate acquaintance with people I might otherwise never have met. She expanded it, too, by giving me the feeling of belonging, so that in my classroom, I felt as if somehow my Black students and I were knit together by bonds that no one but me knew existed. Although I am no longer in an interracial relationship, feelings of belonging did not simply end when the relationship did. The feelings of having been "established *as if* native" in a group other than my birth group are still with me. They show up at times, but only inside me now, most of the time unbeknownst to the people around me, Black, White, or Brown.

Something clutched up inside me when I gave Tineesha that failing grade. I experienced the *zig* of being the teacher, the one in authority, the one obligated to hold all my students accountable. On top of that, I was acutely aware that my skin says, "White."

I also experienced the *zag* of my naturalized self. I'm not suggesting that, by a process of naturalization, I have somehow become the opposite of an Oreo. What would that be, anyway? It turns out that Nabisco now makes a White Fudge Covered Oreo—white on the outside, two layers of black, and a core of white. But I wouldn't for a minute claim that any part of me is Black on the inside. Rather, I've had to admit to myself that I want for my Black students, more than any of the others, that they do themselves proud, do us all proud, be on time, not do anything that would give anyone around them the slightest excuse for believing in stereotypes. I know that when I express this desire, I expose myself as someone asking near perfection of them. I know that doing so is a completely unfair expectation, even a form of discrimination.

Most of the African American students I've taught, like Tineesha, have been female. Despite my admission, what remains of my naturalization makes me long to say to them with gentleness and fierceness what Lucille Clifton wrote to her daughters:

> i command you to be
> good runners to go with grace
> go well in the dark and
> make for high ground
> my dearest girls
> my girls my more than me...

I want for my Black female students, "my dearest girls," what I want for my own daughter, who is not Black, that they be "my girls my more than me," that they settle for nothing less. And I am silenced, because my naturalized self lies so far beneath the surface that it cannot be seen or heard. Yet I am quite sure that these are the words, or something very like them, that Neale would say if she could take my place for a moment.

A Good Stranger

I. SUMMER LULLABY

On summer evenings as a child, I lay in bed and looked out at the massive heap of boulders across from the mission. My eyes touched certain rocks each night, always coming to rest on the huge flat block that had tumbled down eons before, like Lucifer from heaven, separated from the gigantic guardians at the top of the mound. It lay on its side, glowing the color of a ripe apricot in the last light, then turning a dark purple-brown. I held that rock in my vision until my eyes grew heavy. Drowsing, I listened to the opening strains of the lullaby on the hilltop.

The song began with drums booming a deep solemn cadence, followed by chanting, slow and low in the beginning, becoming high-pitched, wild and insistent. I drifted off. When I woke in the middle of the night, the ululations still beat the air, and I wondered if I had slept at all. I felt a fierce surge in my chest, accompanied by guilt, because my parents wanted this summer song, this Diné ceremony, to end. The people my parents hoped to convert were the ones who offered me the first inkling that there could be more than one pathway to the Infinite.

II. SABBATH

Strict Calvinists, Dutch Reformed missionaries in the Navajo Nation, raised me. In many ways, as I would later try to explain, it was like growing up Orthodox Jewish with Christ thrown in. Being Dutch was part of being Christian, just as ethnicity is part of being Jewish. Of my seven brothers, the third generation born in this country, only one has married a woman who isn't Dutch American. Of course, the part about Christ being thrown in isn't quite right, because Christ was not a minor figure. Also, we were missionaries, and Judaism is not a proselytizing religion.

In our own way, we kept the Sabbath as Orthodox Jews do. My mother peeled potatoes for Sunday dinner on Saturday nights to avoid working on the Sabbath. On Sundays, we weren't allowed to ride bikes. Recently, I learned of a public figure whose Orthodox rabbi father destroyed her brother's bicycle because he rode it on the Sabbath. We couldn't play with the neighbor kids, read comics, or play baseball on the Sabbath. We did not buy things, because it would be wrong to cause anyone else to work. We went to church at least twice, sometimes three times, on Sundays and once during the week.

We breathed the Bible, memorized verses and chapters, often by default just because we heard them so often. While we ate, we parsed and analyzed scripture to ensure that we obeyed every commandment exactly as God intended. Then after every meal we read scripture, too. Childhood dinner conversations with my father remind me today of Chaim Potok's characters dissecting Torah and Talmud over a meal. Like us, they tried to determine how the law must be observed.

My paternal grandfather belonged to the Nederduitsers, an even stricter, more cheerless Calvinist sect than ours. I recall a meal where my father and I discussed one of Grandpa's arcane beliefs.

"We got a letter from Grandpa today. He's saying it's a sin for us to have a cross hanging in the chapel. Why would he say that?" my father asked.

Without missing a beat, I answered, "Because to him it's a graven image. The First Commandment says, 'Thou shalt not make unto thee any graven image.'"

"Do you think he's right?"

"Well, Moses made the brass serpent so the Israelites who were bitten by snakes could look at it and be healed. The serpent was a graven image, and God was the one who told Moses to make it. I think the point of the commandment is that we shouldn't put any images above God in our hearts. So, if the cross isn't more important to us than God, it's okay."

My father approved.

III. A CLOAK OF SUBSTANCE

I run naked in the early dawn light. The cool air rushes past my body, and I feel good, until I start to worry that people will see. Then I notice that an orange towel is wrapped around my hips, making me feel safer.

I come to a church whose floors glow a deep blood red. The orange towel now covers my breasts, too. I find myself in the church basement, where people are singing the old hymn, "Out of My Bondage," and I join in, my voice rich and sonorous.

Later, a young man gives us stacks of gospel pamphlets. He announces, "A neighborhood near the church is in trouble. We're going to distribute these to help them out."

Now I want to leave. My body has changed clothing again. I wear a navy skirt and white blouse. I'm hefting a Bible. I pretend I'm about to throw up by covering my mouth and retching, and I race up the stairs and out of the building. Once outside, I can barely move my legs, and I long for the joyous, powerful running from the beginning of my dream. I feel anxious, afraid the young man will follow me and see that I'm not really sick. I can hardly move at all.

A few weeks before this dream, I had decided to devote my summer writing to defining my religious identity. After leaving our church, I had spent twenty-seven years trying to avoid believing in anything. On the first page of my new journal I wrote, "I feel that I know less than I have ever known, that I am an untethered astronaut, adrift in the cosmos. I want to know, not an objective Truth, because I don't think one exists. But I want to know my own mind, my own experience. I want to leave behind the nebulous clouds in which I've clothed myself. I will instead take on a cloak of substance, one that I can feel and others can see."

IV. FIRST *SEDER*

My sophomore year of college, I lived with a Jewish family, and that spring I took part in my first Passover Seder with Sylvia and Abe. I knew the Passover story as told in the book of Exodus. I could name the ten plagues in order without hesitation. I had been taught that the moral of the story was twofold: failure to obey God's commands could result in severe, even fatal, consequences; and the Jews were God's special people.

While brisket bubbled in the oven, Sylvia chopped apples and walnuts to make haroset. I made a salad, and she arranged a shank bone, a hard-boiled egg, a dish of horseradish, saltwater, parsley, and the haroset on a platter. I placed matzah, the unleavened bread that I'd learned about in Exodus, into a basket lined with a napkin. Matzah ball soup simmered on the stove.

At the table, I learned that haroset stood for the mortar the people of Israel had used as slaves in Egypt. Saltwater symbolized their tears, parsley the new life of spring. Abe and Sylvia's youngest niece read the four questions from the *Haggadah*. We drank sweet, dark Manischewitz and sang "Dayenu," the explosion of gratitude that says, "It would have been enough." Fifteen stanzas sing the joy of liberation—"If he had brought us out of Egypt, it would have been enough....If he had split the Red Sea, it would have been enough." When the meal and the questions and the wine and the singing were done, the children searched for the hidden afikomen, the matzah that had been broken in half to be found and eaten after dessert.

Ritual touches the imagination and the emotions, leading to a depth of spiritual experience that the intellect cannot provide. Throughout the meal and long afterwards, I reflected on the significance of the food, the words, the music, and the people with whom I had joined. In church, I had sung a hymn that went, "When I see the blood, I will pass, I will pass over you." I had been taught that this was the Christian extension of Passover—Jesus' blood causing the Angel of Death to pass over us believers. After my first Seder, Passover meant something deeper and older than that. It was as if the food and the wine, no longer mere symbols, had in some ineffable way become part of me.

V. MY DINNER WITH THE *REBBETZIN*

I asked my friend Lakme if she would come for dinner, and if we could talk about how it had been for her to convert to Judaism. I had waited a long time to ask, afraid she might be offended, afraid of what it could mean in my life. She was delighted, and I was nervous.

I'd met Lakme and Gershon, her rabbi husband whose profession made her the rebbetzin, in rural New Mexico, where they were starting a retreat center. Living in a collection of villages and rural stretches with a population of 3,000 at the outside, I had laughed when the postmistress first mentioned "our rabbi." I thought she was joking. Not too long afterwards, I met them at a New Year's Eve dinner.

That spring Lakme and Gershon invited my daughter and me to Seder in their old adobe house, nestled in a rinconcito of pink, gray and yellow walls that led to rocky mesa tops. It seemed an unlikely spot to be celebrating Passover, and in the home of a rabbi, no less. It was the place where the tiny mud-and-stone El Oratorio de Jesus Nazareno had lately been home to cross-bearing, self-flagellating Catholic Penitentes. Close by, Native American Church members planted their tipis and awaited sacred visions.

During the Seder, Gershon departed from the *Haggadah* to offer additional teachings. One of them struck home. "The Hebrew name for Egypt is Mitzrayim, the Land of Narrows," he said, "When the children of Israel left The Land of Narrows, they entered The Wilderness. The Wilderness belongs to no one; hence, it is a place for everyone. This is to show us that spiritual teachings do not belong to anyone. No one group can lay claim to them."

I savored those words. More shared Seders and other Jewish family rituals passed before I invited Lakme to dinner. Only later did I realize that my invitation contrasted with what Gershon had said

Crevice 113

about spiritual teachings belonging to no one. I had asked Lakme because I *wanted* to lay claim to something, to be part of a faith community, to belong.

VI. THE TIE THAT BINDS

There is a place in New Mexico where the red rocks flow like great splendorous waves, a red sea on the high desert. The waves move in and out, in and out, different shades in varied light—red-gold at sundown with a tinge of melancholy at the edges, wine red after rain, soft pink at dawn.

Just before my senior year of high school, the alumni of the Reformed Bible Institute gathered with their spouses and children for a picnic beneath those massive waves, salmon in color on that particular day. We ate food that people eat in Michigan—Jell-O salad, baked beans, potato salad. And we ate foods that most folk in the Midwest had never seen or tasted—Navajo fry bread, mutton ribs, and mutton stew. Some of the Institute's alumni were Diné. The rest were Dutch American and Dutch Canadian.

As always, Ella Descheenee whispered my secret Diné name in my ear and giggled and hugged me. Ella had known me since I was a baby because her husband Ed was my father's mentor at the Bible Institute. In Diné culture, you are not supposed to say your secret name to anyone else, but I can say the English meaning, "Girl Who Reaches After Things." Growing up, I thought it was about being a grabby toddler, but maybe it is also about curiosity, desire and will. What I know for sure is that Ella loved me.

At the end of our picnic, we stood together in a small knot at the edge of an arroyo that cut into the earth between the waves. The leftover food had been packed into pickup truck beds and station wagons. We sang, and our voices echoed off the rocks:

Crevice 114

Blest be the tie that binds
Our hearts in Christian love;
The fellowship of kindred minds
Is like to that above.

There are ways in which, like it or not, I will always be bound by that tie.

VII. ENOUGH CHUTZPAH

After my dinner with Lakme, she told me her conversion story. It began with a dream that, like mine, took place in a church basement. Unlike mine, hers was a vision of knowing without a doubt who she is and always has been—a Jew. Certain in that knowledge, she began the formal conversion process.

When Lakme had finished, I took a deep breath and told her that I had been thinking for years of converting. I tried to convey my motivation, starting with the similarities between my upbringing and my perception of Orthodox Judaism. I talked about the stories from the Old Testament that had nourished me in childhood. We had identified with the Israelites of those stories; they were God's Chosen People, and so were we. I was taught that the Jews who were maligned in the New Testament were not the everyday people, but the politicians, who had acted as politicians ever have. I talked about how Jewish teachings from Lakme and Gershon had opened my heart and returned the Book to me in a way that I loved. I told her about living with Sylvia and Abe, about my first Seder and how important ritual is to my soul. I also told her about a deep-seated fear that I could never truly belong.

Lakme agreed that it took chutzpah to convert. Laughing, she told me that a potential convert to Judaism must be asked three times why they are converting. "It's just supposed to be three times total," she said. "But it seemed like every Jew I knew had to ask me three times."

My heart sank; I didn't know if I could muster the requisite chutzpah.

Lakme is a maggid, a teacher of the sacred. Over dessert and tea, she offered to spend Tuesday evenings with me, exploring the five areas of study required for conversion. I accepted.

Lakme and I met over dinner every other week for five months, and those meals seem now to have coalesced into one long, soul-satisfying dinner with the rebbetzin. Our second meeting stands out because Lakme arrived that night with an armload of books, mostly about Jewish history, and a box of Shabbat candles. History is one of the five areas a person studies in preparation for conversion, and I had asked to start there.

The candles were a pure gift, an invitation, a welcome. Maybe I romanticize Shabbat, remembering the lovely golden glow during candle lighting in the film version of *Fiddler*. But it seems fitting to end the workweek in a spirit of gratitude, of intentional community, in communion over a meal.

VIII. WHO AM I?
When I was small, living in the Navajo Nation in the tiny village of Shiprock, I played in the blazing summer sun with Rudy and Bobby Yellowhair. Every day, we made miniature Diné sheep camps in the dirt. Every day, we began anew, brushing our palms over the camps we had made the day before. I always started with a little rounded hogan, poking a stub of elm twig into the top for a stovepipe and embedding four short twigs on the east side to make a door. Then I broke a bunch of twigs into short, even lengths to make a sheep corral, pushing them into the softened

earth we'd stolen from the edges of my father's squash hills.

I imagined tiny people coming in and out of the hogan to chop wood and cook fry bread. I talked for them, speaking the creole that linguists call Dummitawry English, the language Bobby and Rudy and I used with each other. When Bobby and Rudy switched to Diné bizaad, I recited the Apostles Creed in Diné bizaad. It was the longest piece of spoken Navajo I could manage, and I spoke softly, embarrassed to have Rudy and Bobby hear what I was really saying, but it had to be Diné. I felt poverty-stricken in the language that I needed in order to belong.

IX. TO DANCE WITH OTHERS

I left our church when I was twenty-five. I don't remember any pangs of conscience, and, in the beginning, I felt little grief. There was no joy, either. There was only dying. My soul was like Ezekiel's valley of dry bones, picked clean by vultures and hyenas, bleached white. Then, after seven years of baking in the sun, the dry bones of my soul, took on new flesh through meditation practice. My spirit breathed once more. My connection with God, tenuous at first, grew deeper and more alive than before, unbound by the rules of orthodoxy.

In Ezekiel, after being revived, the valley of bones becomes a great liberation army. In my imagination, the throng danced with the joy of breath blown back into it. Either way, new people came together for a common purpose. As with Ezekiel's bones, reconnecting with God on my own wasn't enough for me; I wanted to join with others. I began to grieve the loss of religious community, the feeling of belonging. The summer I dreamed of running from the church, I set out to recreate what I had lost.

X. WHO DO YOU THINK YOU ARE?

The first time I had other White kids as classmates was at the mission boarding school, when I was eight. I spent most of my time during recess and after school behind the big gray Diné girls' dorm. In the classroom, I used Standard English, but on the playground I automatically switched to Dummitawry English. Playing marbles one day, I called out, "Hey you kits, dit chew saw my rat marvel?"

Katie Van Boven, who had never lived in the Navajo Nation itself, pointed at me, laughing and shouting, "Hey, who do you think you are? You think you're a Navajo or something? You're White, you know. Don't you know that?"

My stomach tightened. Tears threatened to spill. I turned without saying anything, leapt up to the monkey bars and crossed them, three bars at a time, back and forth, back and forth.

XI. AT TEMPLE EMMANUEL

Once in a while, when I lived with Sylvia and Abe, I went to Shabbat services at Temple Emmanuel. The first time, I sat next to Sylvia's mother, a diminutive silver-haired immigrant from Russia. There came a point in the service when everyone turned to greet a neighbor. Ruth turned to me and said, "Good Shabbos," her eyes twinkling. I hesitated and she said, "Come on, you can say it. Good Shabbos."

It wasn't that I couldn't. I was "good" at languages, after all, but I was afraid it might be presumptuous, as if I thought I could be one with them. All I needed was Ruth's encouragement. When I said the words, I was filled with the blessed feeling of belonging.

XII. YÉ'IIBICHEII

Under a blue autumn sky in Shiprock, when it was time for the Northern Navajo Fair, my father prayed, "We ask for rain, Father, that the Yé'iibicheii dances may not be performed, that the people may turn from their heathen practices to serve thee, the only true God." The sky looked nothing like rain, but I knew, of course, that God could work a miracle if he wanted to.

The fair's parade introduced a panoply of color into my black-and-white Dutch Reformed world. Turquoise, gold, scarlet, maroon, hunter green, plum, royal and navy blues, tangerine—satin, velvet or corduroy—shirts, blouses and long gathered skirts. Layers of turquoise and silver—hat bands, squash blossom necklaces, earrings, bolos, bracelets, rings, bow guards, belts and buckles, spurs, trim on bridles and saddles. There were hand-woven saddle rugs, striped Pendleton blankets, green and orange wagons decorated with blankets and juniper greens.

After the parade, we went to the fairgrounds. I smelled mutton ribs, fry bread, and mutton stew. My father bought us kneel-down bread, and I peeled away the rough, damp cornhusks to get to the compact, moist Indian-corn cake. I savored the mild nutty sweetness, rolling each dense bite over my tongue before swallowing. I picked and licked the last crumbs from the narrow crevices of the husk.

To the south of the booths lay the forbidden. I kept looking, knowing it was where the Yé'iibicheii dance would be held. I took on faith my parents' assertion that the ceremony was of the Evil One, but still I wanted to see and hear, to feel the mystery my summer lullabies tendered.

I only saw that place afterwards, when the fair was over. The booths and corrals were empty, the earth packed hard again, and at the south end of the grounds stood rounds of tall juniper branches stuck in the soil, their tips leaning in toward the centers of the circles. Beside them were great orbs of black ash. The green and black rings slipped their magic into my imagination. I closed my eyes and saw a starry sky lit orange by huge leaping bonfires. I saw a crowd of people, wrapped in Pendletons, the ladies with scarves on their heads and men wearing tall black hats, their backs to me, hiding the dancers from my view. I couldn't push through to see, and I heard only silence. I opened my eyes and saw just the wheels of green and black on the hard cream-colored earth.

XIII. ROOTS

Lakme and I began Torah study at my request. I stopped often, needing to talk about my process. Lakme listened, salting her responses with midrash and with the deeper meaning of the original Hebrew.

I talked with her about my efforts to return to my own religious roots and how I had been unsuccessful. Every time someone mentioned Christ, my reaction told me that the flesh had not returned to my spiritual bones with the same hollows and curves as before. I couldn't go back to believing that Jesus was the awaited Maschiach, the Messiah. I saw him now as a gifted rabbi who brought with him the message, "You are all Maschiach. You all have an obligation to redeem the world from destruction, to perform Tikkun Olam." I felt that Christianity was a mistake, that it had departed on an unintended two-thousand-year detour. And there were so many Christian travesties—the Crusades, the Inquisition, pogroms, cultural genocide through worldwide missionary activity—that I abhorred the idea of calling myself Christian.

"Maybe you have to go further back to claim your roots," Lakme suggested.

"You mean to Judaism?"

"Yes."

"I've thought of that," I said.

XIV. GER TOSHAV

Something unexpected happened when, preparing for Torah study, I read the parasha about the original Passover. I had always found it easy to imagine that I was an Israelite, preparing the lamb in a mud hut, sprinkling the doorposts with blood, eating on my feet, dressed for a journey. Reading the story this time was different. I didn't *imagine* being an Israelite; I *was* one. The story was about me. I told Lakme, "This week I read Torah as a Jew. It meant something completely different to me. I can't describe it."

Lakme was delighted. "That's because when you read it as a Jew, you know that God is protecting you."

I hadn't analyzed the meaning, and I still haven't. It was something I experienced, that I felt rather than thought about. The next week I called Lakme to say I needed some distance from the process. I put away everything Jewish and stopped thinking about religious community. For a few weeks. Then books on Jewish spirituality fell off shelves into my hands again. Jewish magazines found their way to my mailbox.

My thoughts had taken a turn, though. I was disturbed to think that possibly I wanted to become a Jew in the same way I'd wanted to be other things I wasn't. I recalled a conversation years earlier with Lily Roanhorse. I'd said, "I'm always careful when I'm with Diné friends because I don't want them to think that I think I know it all, all about Diné life, that is. Sometimes, I hide what I know."

Lily looked straight at me. "You have an identity crisis, just like we do."

Gratitude spread through me, and I nodded. But I felt guilty accepting her recognition. She was too gracious. *We* in her statement referred to college-educated Diné. It wasn't just college that had separated them from their people and ways. The alienation started way back in childhood when they were sent to boarding school. Today mainstream American culture still batters away at Indigenous identity.

"You don't know who you are," Lily said, "and neither do we."

I was so hungry to be seen, to belong, that I didn't argue. But I felt like I was cheating. I knew it was different to be White, wanting to be Brown, even feeling sometimes like I was Brown, and to know acutely that there was no way I ever would be. I knew I benefited from all the privileges our society grants to Whites.

Now, as I considered converting, I had to ask myself if something was missing in me that made me want to be other than self. At this time in the evolution of Earth's peoples, it may be important to cross these distinctions, to become other *and* self, thus one. Today, there is a polar pull between distinctness and unity. Maybe the drive toward distinctness comes from frailty of identity, the deep need to assert who we are. Paradoxically, if we are to cross the lines and create oneness, not out of neurotic need but from a place of strength, it is necessary to first have a strong sense of self.

Despite my curiosity, my feelings for the mystery of my summer lullabies, of the magic circles of the Yé'iibicheii, I have not been drawn to explore Native spirituality. Maybe it's because I had to struggle so hard to establish an identity apart from the Diné world. And in the end, it was the struggle for selfhood that informed my decision about converting to Judaism.

Over the millennia since Abraham and Sarah walked the Middle East, countless people who were not born Jewish have become Jews. I wanted my roots to be Jewish. The late Renewal rabbi, Zalman Schacter-Shalomi, looks at the big picture and says that more people want to convert to Judaism today than have in a long time. He believes it's because the world needs more Jews after the great losses of the Holocaust. For a time, I grasped at that belief to justify my desire.

But I kept returning to the fact that I was not born a Jew. I went back to Lakme and asked her to tell me again about a concept she had mentioned in passing at our first dinner. I thought I remembered an approximate definition, friend to Jews, but I couldn't recall the Hebrew phrase. At the time, I had thought the designation was a pallid substitute for conversion, probably why I forgot the words.

Lakme told me the phrase, *ger toshav*. Its literal meaning, she said, is *good stranger*. It refers to a non-Jew who has the knowledge of what it means to be a Jew. That person would support rather than disrupt Jewish life. A non-Jew who is married to a Jew and is raising his or her children Jewish, without converting, is ger toshav. There is no ceremony for becoming ger toshav; it is something you are, something you can declare yourself to be. I am ger toshav. Some of my deepest spiritual learning comes from Judaism. I celebrate holy days and times with my Jewish friends as often as I am invited.

Ger means *stranger, outsider*. Since my early days in the Navajo Nation, I have worn the identity of an outsider. I have wondered if being ger toshav may not only entail living on the edge of the Jewish community. Maybe claiming to be ger toshav means claiming the religious identity of an outsider, taking on marginality as my spiritual identity. Outsiders have, from time immemorial, served as seers, storytellers, prophets, artists, writers, gadflies, healers, voices crying in the wilderness. If I accept the identity of an outsider, I will not be alone; I will join a great cloud of witnesses, scattered throughout society, who willingly, reluctantly or joyfully live with ambiguity and mystery. It seems that when I ran away from the church in my dream and toward religious identity, the journey took me to where I was all along, back to myself, the destination of all mystical journeys. Happily, it has given me acceptance of myself as an outsider. And it has given me a name for who I am, A Good Stranger.

Tongues

I.

Humans tell stories to explain why Earth is covered by so many tongues. The Tower of Babel is the story I heard as a child. A cautionary tale about folks building a tower into the sky to reach the Holy One. The Holy One got mad because humans were overreaching. Suddenly the builders couldn't understand each other anymore, so they had to stop work. Too many tongues. But why shouldn't we want to touch holiness? With our hearts. With our tongues.

II.

At the Pike Place Market, I stopped to admire the vibrant scarves the artist was laying out on her table. She caressed each silk beauty with her fingers, but for me, it was a tongue thing. "I want to lick them," I said.

"Then they're doing what I want them to."

We smiled.

Gorgeous colors, gleaming smoothness—round and glossy beads, jewels, small stones from beside a trail. They all look so licking-delicious. There must be some neurons that link the pathways between the eyes and the tongue.

III.

The tongue is an organ formed of eight muscles in humans. Four of them are attached to bone, and four are not. We share the presence of this organ with all other tetrapods—four-legged beasts. The tongue is replete with nerves and blood vessels, and its surface is covered with papillae, the tiny bumps we call tastebuds. It is the main organ of our sense of taste, and it enables digestion by helping us chew. It empowers humans to speak and four-leggeds to vocalize.

IV.

I played trombone in high school and college and for a while afterwards. Inserting the tongue repeatedly and rapidly into a brass instrument's mouthpiece creates separate notes on a sustained tone. It's the same with a digeridoo, the long, hollowed, wooden instrument made and decorated with pointillist paintings by Australian Indigenes. I had one once, and it was made from a long, hardened section of hollowed cactus. Having played trombone helped me learn my digeridoo, and tonguing into it had the same effect––breaking up drone notes into short bursts. Played well (by others, I might add) the music raises goosebumps on my skin.

V.

The average human tongue in men weighs about 2.5 ounces, and in women, about 2.1. For such a small organ, it performs a hefty load of work. It is an organ of sense, of connection through language and human intimacy. Oh, for a thousand tongues to sing the praises of the tongue.

VI.

So much of my life is about language and always has been. Different tongues pique my curiosity: How have they been formed? How do people use them or not use them? My parents used Dutch to exclude——when they didn't want us to know what they were talking about. My identity is wrapped up in tongues and in the spaces between tongues. Human identity is ever bound to our Mother Tongue. Having language is about connecting, communicating, knowing people more deeply. The purpose of language is not exclusion.

Diné who don't know me, when they realize, I am not even close to being a fluent speaker, considerately switch to US English—another way of using language. My friends who know that I have some knowledge, speak both US English and Diné bizaad when they're with me. The minuscule size of my little bag of Diné words is a reflection of the In Between identity I struggle to embrace.

VII.

I have in my possession a bag of tongues. I imagine it is a bag I have sewn from a royal blue and orange and green Pendleton blanket. In this bag, lie my two most well-developed tongues—US English and Danish.

The tongue I wish I knew fully is Diné bizaad. When my Diné friends were denied their language, it was denied me, too. Government and mission policies made it so I couldn't learn the language from my peers.

When we take something from one group of people, everyone loses.

I can read German, so it's also in my bag of tongues. I used to be able to speak it. I can read

Norwegian because it's so similar to Danish. I understand quite a bit of spoken Swedish but can barely read it, which shows how differently we may pack diverse tongues into our language bags.

I traveled to Poland because I needed to see Auschwitz. While I was there, I picked up a tiny bag of ten Polish words. In New Zealand, I learned a few Maori words. I read a lot of Jewish literature and lived with a Jewish family once, so I know a smattering of Yiddish. High school Latin helps me with Spanish.

VIII.
Our tongues are attached to the floor of the mouth by the frenulum, a mucous membrane. When the frenulum is too short and too thick, it renders speech, eating, and swallowing difficult. We say someone with that kind of frenulum is tongue-tied. The solution is to snip the frenulum to loosen the tongue.

On the other hand, tongue-tied is when you can't find your words.

By contrast, a teller of secrets has a loose tongue. Too many words.

IX.
The Latin word for "tongue" is "lingua," which is also the Latin word for "speech." Many everyday English words come from "lingua"—language, linguist, lingual, bilingual, multilingual, cunnilingus, lingo, to name a few.

X.
My mother was rarely given to silliness, but sometimes we would tease her, and then she would

stick out her tongue at us, and we would all laugh. Her, too.

After living in New Zealand, which the Maori call *Aotearoa*, The Land of the Long White Cloud, I am always deeply moved when I hear and watch the Maori *haka*. The haka is a group war dance or challenge. It touches me most profoundly when it is performed to honor someone of warrior character— for instance, when a firefighter has died. Their companions execute a haka for them. Loud, energetic chanting and roaring are accompanied by the dramatic sticking out of tongues. It can show prowess, challenge, intimidation, bravery, or honor.

XI.
My Mother Tongue is the US variety of English. I also heard Dutch and Diné bizaad before I left my mother's womb. Dutch from my father's parents and sometimes from my mother and father. Diné bizaad from the Diné man who was my father's big brother, his mentor, at Bible School, and especially from Ed's wife, Ella, who talked more than Ed.

XII.
The church of my youth was not a shouting church. Members scoffed at Pentecostal churches, where people spoke in tongues. "Holy Rollers," they called them. Once, when I was ten years old, I went to that kind of church with my friend. It was loud and mysterious, fervid. The worshippers were heirs of the biblical apostles who had tongues of fire land on their heads at Pentecost. All that emotion scared me, but I sure hoped I would get to see tongues of fire.

XIII.
The tongue of a cow makes a delicious sandwich. It's been a long time since I saw a beef tongue in the meat section of a supermarket, but one place I shop has real, live butchers, and I can purchase a tongue if I ask. A cow tongue weighs three to four pounds. I bring one home and simmer it in salted water with lemon slices, cloves, coriander seeds, and peppercorns. When it is tender, which comes after hours of cooking, I slice it thin, and the slivers are smooth on my tongue.

XIV.
The tongues we speak bring us the taste of words. The muscles wrap themselves around teeth and cheeks and lips to make the sounds. The tongues we speak also present us with lavish food flavors. From US English, mac and cheese. When I am being Dutch-American, I eat *moes*, a peasants' mix of mashed potatoes or rice with bacon fat, kale, and bacon pieces. At Christmas, my grandmother mailed us the flaky, buttery, Dutch almond pastry, *banket*. In Diné bizaad, I can never get enough *dahdíníilghaazh*—puffy golden fry bread and with it, mutton stew. My friend Pita says my *ris alamande*, the Danish Christmas rice pudding, made with almond slivers, whipped cream, and cherries, is food from the gods. In Jewish homes, at Passover, I eat brisket and matzoh ball soup, charoset, and bitter herbs.

XV.
When she was in middle school, my daughter asked if she could get her tongue pierced. I had by then learned that it was useful to say no by saying yes—

little to no resistance from a teen. So I said, "Yes, but you will have to save enough money ahead of time for the piercing and for treating any infections that could result." She never brought it up again.

XVI.
Conquerors, colonizers, and occupiers the world over have, through concerted effort, including physical and cultural violence, erased Indigenous tongues. Irish Gaelic and Scottish Gaelic were nearly eradicated by the takeover of the British colonizers. It happened through violence, through the perceived prestige of speaking English, and sometimes through more benign intercultural contact. Scottish Gaelic is now an endangered language. Irish Gaelic is making a comeback through revitalization efforts.

XVII.
I dream sometimes that I am speaking Diné bizaad fluently with one of my friends. I feel overjoyed. Then, before the dream is over, I realize I am speaking Danish, the only language other than US English in which I am fluent. The power of my disappointment wakens me every time.

XVIII.
In Chinese medicine, the tongue is used to diagnose health problems. Is the tongue coated? What color is the coating? Does the tongue tremble when at rest? Are there tooth impressions on the sides of the tongue? Once, when a Chinese medicine doctor had been treating me for a while, as always, she took a look at my tongue and exclaimed, "Oh! What's

happened?" She went to work right away prescribing a new set of horrible-tasting herbs for me to make into a foul-smelling tea.

XIX.
Throughout the US, the government and missionaries have tried to obliterate Indigenous languages. For more than a century, the speaking of US English was forced on school children. They were severely punished for speaking their Mother Tongue.

The United Nations Educational, Scientific and Cultural Organization (UNESCO) estimates that half of the approximately 6,000 tongues spoken around the globe today are in danger of disappearing. By UNESCO standards, Diné bizaad is one of them.

The *UNESCO Atlas of the World's Languages in Danger* asks, "Why preserve language diversity?" In the Diné Language Teachers' Association (DLTA) handbook for a Diné language revitalization project, Louise Benally gives this answer: "Diné bizaad and, through it, the cultural beliefs and practices that it imparts, is valuable because it is our identity. It makes us who we are. We have pride in the teachings, the beliefs, and the traditional songs and stories that provide us the foundation for being a Diné person. When we listen to Diné bizaad, it makes us feel good. It brings us home. When we listen to a Diné song, it moves us to cry, to laugh or just to be silent in awe."

XX.
The desire to lick things that are not food must be what makes adults tell children not to lick a metal pipe in winter. Otherwise, why would anyone even think of it? A tongue frozen to a pipe is consequently

forever fixed within the repertoire of slapstick humor. Has anyone ever done it in real life?

XXI.
And why is a wagon tongue even called a tongue? Who first named it that? I haven't been able to find out.

XXII.
Tongues eating, speaking, playing, grant us sampling tongues, twisting tongues, coding tongues, frozen tongues, lashing tongues, flaming tongues, reclaiming tongues, sly tongues and honest tongues, faltering tongues, silver tongues, licking tongues. (Fashioned after Ross Gay on "skateboarding eyes" in *Inciting Joy*)

The Importance of Clear

"Often it is not we who shape words
but the words we use that shape us."
~Nina George, *The Little Paris Bookshop*

I. PLAYING IN DUMMITAWRY ENGLISH
In 1952, our family lived in Shiprock, a village in the
Navajo Nation. We lived there because my father was
a missionary, something I told people with pride until
my early twenties. Something I didn't want to admit
for a long time after that. We lived in a large two-story
house on top of a hill that overlooked Jack's Trading
Post. On that same hilltop, not far from the house that
the mission board provided, lived my first Diné
playmates, Bobby and Rudy Yellowhair. Every day the
boys and I met in a spot of shade between my father's
garden and a small wooden garage. My father had
spread apricot and peach halves on the garage roof to
dry. Every once in a while, a breeze brought us the
faint sweetness of drying fruit.

We stole soft dirt from my father's squash and
melon hills, and from it we created miniature Diné
home sites. We snapped thin elm twigs into short
pieces and poked them upright into the dirt to form
corrals. Tiny pebbles inside the fold became our sheep
and goats. A little pile of earth with a bit of twig
pressed into the top for a stovepipe became a hogan—
a traditional Diné home. Outside the hogan, we
heaped dried, platinum-colored grass to make an

outdoor cook fire. Finally, we peopled our homes with imaginary characters, and then we talked for them.

We started off speaking what linguists have called *Dummitawry English*. At that time, most Diné who spoke English used this creole, which meant speaking English with a Diné accent sprinkled here and there with Diné words. Often it also included modified syntax. At some point in our play, the Yellowhair brothers would almost always switch to speaking Diné bizaad. I might not notice at first, but when I did, I felt poverty-stricken; I owned only a small bag of Diné words. I closed my mouth for a little while. Then, under my breath I started speaking the longest bit of Navajo I knew—the Apostles Creed. I just wanted the boys to be able to hear that I was speaking Diné bizaad; I didn't want them to hear my actual words because I was ashamed of what I didn't know. I repeated the creed again and again, imagining the little mother flipping fry bread and laying it in a pan on the cook fire. As she told stories to her children, I was saying, "God ataa' t'áá bí t'éiyá alaahgo..." I believe in God, the Father Almighty... .

II. SPEAKING DINÉ COMES WITH K'É

It had been easy for me to start speaking Dummitawry English. I was learning to speak Diné bizaad at the same time, but that involved conscious thought. In the Diné worldview, every person, every animal, every star, is related—connected through a kinship system called *k'é*. I caught on to the most elementary k'é as I learned the language. When I greeted someone in Diné bizaad, using the right kinship term was simply part of it. If a woman was old enough to be my grandmother, I called her *shimásání*. If she was my mother's age, she was *shimá*.

I became versed in small social skills, like shaking hands with a soft passing of palms, rather than the firm clasp-and-shake of the dominant culture. I could see that my father was proud of me, and Diné who visited our home laughed with apparent pleasure when I served them coffee and spoke Diné bizaad to ask what they took in it. "Abe' nínízinísh? Áshiiłikan sha'?" I was pleased, too.

During our first summer in Shiprock, my father went away to learn how to read the Diné language. Early missionaries had created a Navajo alphabet, wanting people to read the Bible for themselves. Later, the Diné-Bilagáana linguistics team, William Morgan and Robert Young, refined and standardized the written language. When my father came back from his training, he could read the Navajo New Testament from the pulpit pretty well, and he could teach others to read. He taught me at the same time I was learning to read English. I thought this was the natural order of things. More accurately, I probably didn't think about it. Like the rest of my life, it just happened back then, the way life does for children. Our lives don't seem special or unusual because they are ours and we are perhaps more present in them than we will be at any other time. Though I wasn't aware of it, reading in Diné bizaad helped increase my vocabulary. My father's mission thus became some of my earliest lessons in a language that would surround me and return to me for the rest of my life, though it would never be fully part of me.

III. MY MOTHER, THE LANGUAGE COP
Less than a year after we settled in Shiprock, our family moved to Teec Nos Pos, deeper within Dinétah. This tiny place was close to the Four Corners—the exact spot where the states of Arizona, Colorado, New Mexico and Utah meet. I kept on building tiny Diné home places, now on the floor of the sandy bottom of the arroyo across from the mission. I played with my

brothers and sister and with Sally and Carol Belone whose mother was the matron at the Bureau of Indian Affairs (BIA) School. I kept on speaking Dummitawry English with my friends and classmates.

Sometimes Dummitawry English slipped out at the dinner table. One of us might say, "Pass da brat, please."

My mother, a vigilant language cop, would correct us immediately. "You mean, 'Pass the bread please.'"

"Ja."

"Say it." We did.

She corrected little oddities we picked up at school. We all called the tallest of my friends Mareeta. "I'm sure her name is supposed to be Marietta," Mom said when she heard me talking about her.

"No, it's Mareeta."

But when Mareeta came for cake and ice cream when I turned seven, my mother called her Marietta. Mareeta, of course, had no idea who she was talking to.

I brought a game home from school and taught it to my sister and brothers. "Whoever's it says, 'Rilla, rilla, rilla, I see something. It is rat. What is it?'"

"You mean, 'Riddle, riddle, riddle. I see something *red.*'"

I conceded to red instead of rat, as we would say it in Dummitawry English. But, "No. It's rilla, rilla, rilla."

I was interested in language, in traversing more worlds than one, although at the time I saw both worlds as part of my one world, my only world. I have no doubt that I would have become fluent in Diné bizaad on the playground except for the language policies in the schools in the Navajo Nation. Speaking Diné bizaad, even when children came to school with no knowledge of English, was forbidden. Teachers and dormitory matrons punished children if they caught them speaking their own language. The most natural and efficient way for children to learn a second language is from their peers, so at the same time my friends' language was being ripped from them, I was being denied access to that language. I would feel that loss keenly as the years passed. My loss, however, would never be as great a loss as Diné children's was. Knowing how my insufficiency paled next to the costs my friends paid set me further apart from people to whom I wanted deeply to belong.

IV. WHITE LANGUAGE, WHITE SKIN

In 1957, when I was eight, my parents sent me to mission boarding school, 135 miles from home. It was the first time I had classmates who were White. One day, during recess, we were out on the playground by the dorms. It was spring, and we were playing marbles. It was my turn to shoot, and I couldn't find my red cat eye shooter. I called out in my best Dummitawry English "Hey, you kits, ditchyou saw my rat marvel?"

Katie Van Boven, a White girl who lived at the mission with her parents and had never lived in the Nation, hooted. "Hey, what did you just say?" Her laughter had a mean edge. "Who do you think you are? You think you're a Navajo? You're not Navajo. You're White. You know that?"

I looked around at my friends, who were Diné. They kept their eyes on the ground, studying the marbles in the circle. I felt my face flush and clenched my hands. I stopped looking for my shooter and jumped up from the marble circle. I brushed the dirt and pebbles from my knees and ran to the monkey bars. I traveled across and back, across and back, three-at-a-time. I swallowed hard against the thick saltiness in my throat.

After that day, I took care to notice who was around when I spoke and which form of English I used. Sometimes I slipped into Dummitawry English without realizing it, but never again so heavily around the other White kids. I thought of the Diné kids as my real friends. At the same time, I began to admit to myself that I wasn't one of them.

I started to want to belong to the secretive, tightly woven group of White missionaries' kids, the ones who had never lived in the Nation but always on the main mission campus, where the school was. I felt ashamed for wanting it. I asked myself why I should wish to belong to a group that excluded me and was mean to me. I excused my longing by telling myself that my Native friends all went home from boarding school in the summer, and who was left for me if I wasn't part of the White group? But I never broke into that knot of whiteness.

I felt an In Between ache that wouldn't go away. Some part of me thought that because I looked like those White kids, I must be part of them. At the same time, my heart held an opposite, even more impossible longing—to be Diné. As time went on, I created fantasies in which I had been born mixed—Diné and Bilagáana I cradled those stories to myself and dwelled on them over and over.

V. A TWO-LANGUAGE LIFE
After high school, I left for our church college in Michigan. We had visited relatives there some summers, but that was different from living and going to school there. I was rammed into culture shock in that green-treed, gray-skied, Dutch-American world. I never fit in, and after two years, I transferred to the University of New Mexico. At UNM, the Diné language was offered as a university subject, and in those classes, a systematic approach gave me an appreciation for the tremendous intricacies of the language. My natural next step was to study

linguistics and the field of bilingual education, which took me onto a career path that fit with my early life.

Because of the Bilingual Education Act of 1968, Navajo Nation schools had started to teach children to read and write and do science, math, and social studies in Diné bizaad. To do this, teachers needed vocabulary that hadn't previously existed in Diné bizaad. New colors joined the Diné spectrum. Teachers needed to know what to call a parallelogram. As a graduate student, I was hired to travel from one bilingual teacher training program in Dinétah to another, recording the terminology teachers were trying out, working to help standardize nomenclature among the schools. Until then, no one had talked about the color purple in the Diné language; the new word became *tsídídééh*, the name for the wild purple four o'clock flower. "Triangle" became *táá'go deez'á*, meaning "three-pointed."

Bilingual education grew into a movement, and the government funded bilingual publishing houses around the country. Most were for Spanish programs; the only Native one was located in Albuquerque. People on staff were mostly Indigenous—artists, writers, educators, linguists, and the Diné half of the creators of the *Navajo-English Dictionary* then in use. These were highly skilled, creative and innovative people, and I felt lucky to be one of the few White teammates. Our director, a visual artist, poet, and educator from Shiprock, had a master's degree in education from Harvard and was a consummate networker and visionary. She encouraged us to think outside the box. Gone were the rough illustrations on mimeographed paper from which I'd learned to read Diné bizaad. Our center produced four-color, glossy books and posters— materials that legitimized reading and academic learning in the Diné language and made it attractive besides.

Our biggest project was the creation of a full-day curriculum that integrated Diné tradition, language, and learning modalities as vehicles for teaching customary school subjects. The goal was to create Diné graduates who were fully bilingual and bicultural, able to function in many worlds with ease, and accomplished in the unique gifts of their culture.

Before we wrote, we spent days listening to a hataałi—what Bilagáanas call a *medicine man* and literally translates as *singer*—teach us about the Diné cosmos, the astonishingly intricate web that connects all of life. This was when I learned the word *k'é* and realized that I had practiced k'é in a limited way for a long time. I knew now that when old Grandma Begay rocked me to and fro, calling me shitsóí, shitsóí—my granddaughter, my granddaughter—we had been acknowledging k'é together. But now I also saw that there was so much more to k'é than our human connectedness. The constellations were related to cycles of life, corn pollen and sun, thoughts and the Earth. Every. Thing. Related. The complexity of it made me gasp. The hataałi just smiled and nodded at my wonderment. It also became painfully clear to me that this way of seeing the universe, though I really had so little comprehension of it, was what my parents—missionaries—and the BIA had sought to destroy.

From our days of listening to the elder—the singer—a rough outline of the future curriculum evolved. Later, it fell to me to refine, expand and apply the outline to a school setting, then work with Diné teachers to create sequenced lessons. After that, our writing staff refined the lessons further, created accompanying stories, and worked with our art and design department to create visuals for completed curriculum and materials kits.

Our collective zeal was not unlike the passion of my parents and their fellow missionaries. We were living in high times, standing at the forefront of a movement that we thought could turn the tide of cultural losses—losses that were becoming more and more rapid and far-reaching. I realized, dimly at first, that I was, on some level, trying to repair the damage I felt my parents had inflicted. And I began to be aware of wanting to atone for being White.

At the same time, I longed for the place that means home to me—Teec Nos Pos. I remembered the beating drums and chanting voices, starting low and slow, growing high and passionate on the hill above the mission—my summer lullabies. In addition to the confusion of being White Not Diné, I knew I could not go home again to Teec Nos Pos or any part of the Navajo Nation. Not to live. What had once been home was now Home Not Home.

VI. WALKING AWAY FROM THE GIFT
Even as I entered more deeply into knowledge of the Diné worldview, even as I hoped our shared work in the bilingual education movement would repair some of the damage that had been done for well over a century, I began to sense that I would need to go even farther away from home—the home that no longer existed—in order to find home within myself. One evening, after a long day of training kindergarten teachers to use our bilingual-bicultural kit, Lily Roanhorse and I sipped cold drinks in the lounge of the Farmington Holiday Inn. Lily got to talking about what it was like to be college-educated Diné, how it put her and others into an in-between place, always trying to figure out where they belonged.

As we talked, I said something about how, if I was in a group with Diné, I often hid what I knew of the language and ways. "I don't want to overstep or act like I think I know more than I do." The underlying message was, "I don't want to be guilty of appropriating something that doesn't belong to me."

I am still moved by the gift of grace that Lily extended to me in that moment. "You have an identity crisis just like we do," she said. "We don't know who we are, and neither do you."

I was so grateful to be seen by her, even though I knew it wasn't the same. I might question where I fit in, just as Lily did, but I was still White. I could avail myself anytime of all the privileges that came with my skin.

I left Diné education because I believed that Diné children deserved Diné teachers and Diné leaders. I felt this was the right order of things, even when another of my teammates in the publishing house, Ilene, told me I could contribute something unique to the work we were doing. "You know the culture from inside and outside," she said. "It means you have a different perspective. We need different perspectives."

Ilene and I shared an office, but we'd known each other since childhood. We had eaten fry bread together in her mother's hogan, and we had played house, pretending to be members of a tribe neither of us belonged to. Later, we graduated in the same class from the mission school and attended some of the same courses at the university.

Despite what Lily and Ilene said and how much I respected them, despite how grateful I was for what they saw in me, I had to leave. In retrospect, I see that leaving had as much to do with my need to find out who I really was as it did with my vision of Diné educators for Diné students. Both women had offered me a place, a niche, but at the time, I couldn't embody the vision; I couldn't claim it.

VII. IDENTITY COMING AND GOING
In my first move away from things Diné, I trained to be a clinical counselor. Then I left the high desert

altogether and traveled and lived in far-flung places—first San Francisco, then Copenhagen, southern Sweden, a farm near the northernmost tip of New Zealand, then back closer to home, just south of Santa Cruz, California. And, at last, I found my way back to a spot on the eastern edge of Diné Country. I pieced together several different jobs as a counselor in the tiny rural community of Cuba, New Mexico.

Torreon is a Diné community close to Cuba, and I found work there in the BIA school and in the community at large. The present school is a modern cinderblock building, but the old school was still standing, and it housed Headstart and parent programs. Depression era work projects had built schools all over Dinétah, using native stone and pine logs. The schools looked pretty much alike, so when I entered the one at Torreon, I felt I as if I were back in my school at Teec Nos Pos. I experienced a sense of familiarity, of homecoming, and also some of the anxiety I had felt in my first school.

The school at Torreon smelled the same as my old one—like red sawdust sweeping compound, linoleum, Vaseline, and government commodity cheese. I guess I could say it was the smells that brought out the Dummitawry English in me. But really, it was being with people. By then, I had experienced myself in so many different contexts that I had more of a sense of who I was. I was more solidly me. But I couldn't help noticing that when I crossed the line into Dinétah, singing welled up inside me. I smiled to myself when I had to stop for a herd of sheep to cross the road. I drank in the mesas and juniper and sage. And I slipped without noticing it back into that different way of speaking. My accent wasn't as strong as when I'd earned Katie Van Boven's scorn, but it was there. My way of joking changed, too, when I hit the Nation. I didn't consciously warn myself to guard the newfound sense of who I was. Yet, unconsciously I took care, always staying aware that I wasn't Diné, old fantasies and wishes to the contrary. I was me—an In Between person, but still me.

VIII. HIDING

Sometimes when I was back in the Nation, I noticed that I was an invisible me, and much of that was my own doing. At one point, I contracted to train Diné counselors in a substance abuse program near Cuba. During that time, our staff traveled once on business to the Navajo Nation capital in Window Rock. At lunch, our program director ordered a meal of corn, beans and squash. Jean said, in Diné bizaad, that long ago her people had eaten a vegetarian diet like the dish she was eating.

I was surprised, because roast mutton, mutton stew, and fry bread are mainstays of today's traditional menu, and the rest of us were tucking into our mutton stew with gusto. I said, "T'áásh aaníí?"

Jean turned to me. Carefully, slowly, she explained what she had just said about the vegetarian diet, but she said it in English.

In response, I mirrored her, repeating my words, only in English this time—a polite, "Really?" I said it as if I hadn't understood what she'd said in Diné bizaad.

Even though Jean knew that I had grown up in the Navajo Nation and that I understood and spoke some Diné bizaad, when I said, "T'áásh aaníí?" she had relied on the visual cue of my whiteness. She literally did not hear that I had responded in Diné to her Diné. Her overly careful English interpretation of her own words seemed to be an unconscious recognition that something confusing had just happened linguistically, but she apparently had no cognitive or sensory reference points for the event. And I was not about to make any kind of statement about it. I just went with her flow, making myself—my intercultural self—invisible. Jean went on to talk about how, as a child, she'd picked and eaten wild carrots and wild onions. I had done the same thing up on the mountain at Teec Nos Pos. I kept that information to myself, too.

IX. ONE DOWN
Around the time of our staff trip to Window Rock, I discovered the Diné comedian, the late Vincent Craig. Craig had both admirers and critics among Diné, as he liberally used both Dummitawry English and Diné bizaad to get laughs. Because we lived in Cuba, my daughter Cheyenne was getting a small taste of what my growing up years had been like. Many of her classmates were Diné, and she enjoyed our Vincent Craig album almost as much as I did. She definitely got his language-based humor.

One evening we had dinner guests—a couple of Bilagáana friends who brought along a Diné friend of theirs. Something in our conversation reminded Cheyenne of one of Craig's sketches. I wasn't aware yet of how controversial his comedy was; to me it was just the humor of home. So when Cheyenne asked if she could tell one of the jokes, I saw no harm in it. She told it well, but it fell worse than flat. The Diné woman's response was, "Oh, yes. The accent." And one of the Bilagáana women, Kim, took me to task for allowing Cheyenne to tell what she regarded as an oppressive joke.

Kim's comment sliced deep. I didn't understand why my pain was so powerful and thought I must be overreacting. I desperately wanted to correct what felt like a huge misunderstanding. In some vague way, Kim's words reminded me of the marble-playing incident. I called her the day after the dinner and tried to explain that Dummitawry English was a language I'd spoken as a child and that Cheyenne, too, spoke it at times with her classmates.

"That may be, but I'm sure that when you use it, it's with a sense of one-upmanship," Kim said.

With a sinking feeling, I examined myself for racism. For days I grappled with the incident without gaining equanimity.

X. THE IMPORTANCE OF CLEAR

Years later, the understanding I had sought, and so much more, slid into place with a resounding click. I was having breakfast with my friend Alicia, then a doctoral candidate in cross-cultural communication. In the course of our conversation, I used the word *clear*.

Alicia stopped me. "There," she said. "What you just said. That's it!"

"What are you talking about?"

"It's the way you said *clear*."

"*Clear*?"

"Yes, you did it again. You just used an initial voiceless, unaspirated, alveolo-palatal fricative."

I understood her technical terminology from my study of linguistics and my university courses in Diné bizaad. It describes a sound that is made by placing the tip of the tongue behind the front teeth and blowing air past one side of the tongue. It makes the word *clear* sound something like *tlear*.

Alicia went on, "I've heard this different thing in your speech ever since I've known you (for nearly twenty years at that point), but I couldn't put my finger on it before. That's what it is." Her voice carried the triumph of finally having figured out something that had eluded her.

"I say it that way all the time? Not just once in a while?"

"All the time."

All the time. It's something that is a permanent part of me. It doesn't come and go, depending on where I am or whom I'm with, the way Dummitawry English does. Tears sprang to my eyes.

"I know what it is," I said. "It's a sound that occurs in a lot of Diné words, like *ditlee'*. *Ditlee'* means *wet*. Do you know what this means, Alicia?" Now I felt excited.

She smiled and nodded as I said, "This is part of who I am, this little linguistic quirk. It's not something I put on and take off when I'm coming and going into Dinétah."

She nodded again. She did know what it meant.

"I've been completely unaware of it."

"There. You just did it again."

I looked my question. Then, excited I said, "The /pl/ blend in *completely*."

I cradled this word *clear* and began to notice other words that I pronounce that way, like *clean* and *click*. If I work at it, I can choose to pronounce *clear* the way most native speakers of Standard American English do, but it is not the norm for me. I have to think about it, carefully place my tongue in the right place to form the sound that creates this tiny bit of the English language.

I was happy with my new awareness, but after a while I moved on, and I more or less forgot about the importance of *clear*. Then one morning, I was talking to another high school staff member before class. Jamie, a mixed Diné and Laguna student, stood nearby. Suddenly, she interrupted me.

"Hey! You just said *tlear*!"

"Oh. Yeah, that *is* how I say it," I said offhandedly, but I also laughed with pleasure—at myself and at Jamie's recognition of me. I explained how Alicia had told me about my idiosyncrasy. Then I said, "So you heard it, huh?" I didn't try to keep the gratification out of my voice.

Crevice 148

What Ilene and Lily knew, what Jamie heard, what Alicia heard, what they told me, helped me, in the end, to know something of who I am. I am not Diné—that much is obvious in so many ways. Nor am I mainstream American, whatever that is. I am someone else, someone In Between, having an identity of my own. When a child is surrounded by a culture other than the one she was born into, a long fall may be set in motion, pulling her into a cleft that lies deep between two ways of being in the world. I have discovered that if one is able to climb out of that crevice, one may lay oneself across cultural gaps—a bridge among, not only those original cultures, but among other cultures and other peoples, as well.

PART III
PASSAGE

Crevice 152

Racial Injustice Benefited Me

I grew up in the Navajo Nation and in Gallup, New Mexico. My parents were White missionaries. After the murder of George Floyd by a White policeman, we witnessed an outpouring of rightful outrage. Then and now, we are reminded about many others whose lives have been violently ended or damaged only because of their skin color. We see and hear the words, "Black Lives Matter." Some people object, saying "All lives matter." Of course, they do, but not all lives are in danger the way Black and Brown lives are. The signs could well say, "Black and Brown Lives Matter," because in the US, police kill Indigenous people at a higher percentage than any other group. These are the people whose lives are in danger from the people who are supposed to serve and protect them.

As a White woman, I have benefited all my life from being White in the US. This looked a little different in the Navajo Nation from how it might have looked in other parts of the country, but without a doubt I benefited because of my skin color. My family always lived in a house with running water. When we lived deep within the Navajo Nation at Teec Nos Pos, Diné people drove miles with horse and wagon to fill their water barrels. It could take all day to do this, while we simply turned a tap many times a day, thinking nothing of our privilege. Today 30% of Diné homes are still without running water, which has been a major factor in the extreme force COVID-19 exerted in the Navajo Nation.

In 1954, when I started school, Diné children were being forcibly taken from home and sent to government and mission boarding schools, where they were punished for speaking their own language. But what could they speak? Not English. They didn't know English. There were no carefully sequenced lessons to teach English as a Second Language. It was sink or swim. I already knew how, not only to speak English but also to read it. The principal moved me up to second grade on my first day. I had these educational advantages as a day student in that government boarding school because I was White.

On my first day of school, after our lunch of commodity cheese sandwiches and lumpy powdered milk that made me gag, the matron marched us to the dormitory for naps. I knew the matron because her daughters were my playmates. I tried to tell her I didn't take naps anymore, but she acted like she didn't know me and sent me to one of the beds. I thought it meant I would have to stay there night after night, which seemed for always, like all the other children. Never go home again. As soon as the matron left, I rolled off my bed, snuck across the hall, out the heavy metal door, and raced down the hill—home to the mission, sobbing all the way. My mother called the principal and arranged for me to come home for lunch after that. This happened because I was White. The parents of my Diné classmates couldn't speak to the principal in the "right" language. They didn't have telephones. The government forced them into boarding school compliance.

When I was eight, I was sent to mission boarding school. Unlike the parents of my classmates, my parents weren't forced to send me; it was a choice. Because I was White, I went home every other weekend. The Diné children went home once during the school year for Christmas vacation. I was terribly homesick. Diné children were deeply homesick, too, with far more reason—silenced because they didn't know the language, punished for speaking theirs, ripped from land and culture, from all that was sacred to them. Everything but home was familiar for me. I could excel in school simply because of language and cultural knowledge. At the end of that year, my parents moved to Gallup. No more boarding school. They had that choice because we were White.

Once, at our family-style lunch in the mission dining hall, I asked a Diné high school student to pass me the milk—in Diné bizaad. I didn't even think about what I was doing. Years later, he told me he had thought at the time, "If this little White girl can speak Navajo to me, why shouldn't I speak my own language?" Nothing happened to me because I used Diné bizaad. At the end of the school year, that Diné student was told he couldn't leave with his father until he paid 85 cents. "Why?" he asked and was told, "A nickel for every time you talked Navajo." He didn't know he had been observed and charged. In 1957, 85 cents was money his family didn't have.

I have benefited in literally countless ways—— then and still today, simply because my skin is of the inherited pigmentation we call *White*. Not Black or Brown. These are only very few examples.

Being Third

> "The 'third' is that which questions
> binary thinking and introduces crisis."
> ~ Marjorie Garber, *Vested Interests*

It was a cool August morning in Williams, Arizona, and I was about to board the Grand Canyon Railway, courtesy of one of the railway's entertainers. Clarence (Diné) walked me to my coach, and I had put my foot on the lowest step, when he said, "Just a minute. I want to introduce you to someone." As we walked down the line of cars, he said, "She's the first Navajo woman to be hired as a conductor on the line."

Sondra stood beside the doorway to one of the rear cars, professional in her black vest, white shirt and black tie. "I want you to meet a friend of mine," he said to her in English. Then he slipped into Diné bizaad. "T'iis Názbas naaghádéé'."

Sondra's face registered confusion. Here was Clarence telling her that this obviously Bilagáana woman came from Teec Nos Pos, a tiny place in the northeast part of the Navajo Nation.

Her face said, "Bilagáanas don't come from there."

Back to English, Clarence added, "We went to school together."

Now Sondra's face registered understanding.

I smiled and said, "That explains it," letting her know I'd seen her bewilderment and that I'd understood both Clarence's Diné and English words.

"No," she objected, in case I'd thought her uncertainty was rude.

Clarence was clearly enjoying himself. He's a talented musician and a joker who loves poking his finger into stereotypes of all kinds. The three of us chuckled, probably each for different reasons.

I settled into my seat and considered how the young woman had tried to place me, how naturally we try to match a new acquaintance with our binary templates: female-male, gay-straight, old-young, Diné-Bilagáana, Black-White. I thought about a time when I was visiting Alice Whitegoat (Diné). Several of us had gotten together to talk about a Diné bizaad revitalization project; the language is being lost at a rapid rate. Alice introduced me to a retired Diné educator and poet. "Anna's a writer, too," Alice said. "She worked with us at the Native American Materials Development Center in the early days."

"Oh, the token White," was all Inez said.

We went on talking as if she hadn't said anything unusual. As we brainstormed during the morning, I noticed Inez watching me now and then. Finally, during a break, she asked, "What do you write?"

All the other participants knew me, and I think Inez had started to see that I was a valued contributor to our conversation. She heard that I knew some Diné bizaad and quite a bit of linguistics. To me, it seemed that she had begun to think that what I had to offer was more than symbolic, and she'd allowed herself to consider that I might be more than a paper cutout. Maybe she could entertain some interest in me as a person.

Crevice 157

Ella Descheenee knew who I was. She had waited until she knew me to give me my Diné name. Ella knew me from birth because she and her husband attended Bible School with my father in Michigan, where I was born. Near the end of one Sunday dinner, Ella watched me reach as far as I could across my highchair tray, grunting with effort, trying to grab a piece of bread from the big folks' table. She laughed.

"Now I know your name," she said. Only people who are close should know a person's Diné name. In my case, it would always be Ella, her husband Ed, my mother and father. I keep the Diné words to myself as I should, but in English it means something like *Girl Who Reaches After Things*.

Soon after my naming, Ella and Ed took charge of a mission post back in the Navajo Nation. A couple of years later, my father was assigned a post in Shiprock, so we saw them now and then at missionary gatherings. Every time she laid eyes on me, on up into adulthood, Ella drew me into her soft arms. She whispered my name in my ear and giggled. I knew Ella loved me. She knew who I was and watched and waited and cuddled me and all that time looked for *me*. She never looked for a box to put me in.

From a sidewalk in Berkeley, I saw a tall, slender person perusing the contents of a bookshelf. I saw long, straight blondish hair, a rust-red velvet jacket, tight green pants, and butter-colored boots up to the knees. I knew I was staring and that I shouldn't. I found the person highly attractive, but I was looking for curves and bulges that would tell me whether I was seeing a man or a woman. This was decades before the more recent general recognition that there can be a multitude of expressions of gender. Yet even now, the Euro-American conditioning to discern binary gender runs deep, whereas traditional Diné thought includes four genders—feminine female, masculine male, masculine female, and feminine male—all accepted in traditional Diné life.

I've wanted to ask some of my Diné friends, but I never have, "How do you see me? What categories do you sort me into? Bilagáana? Lesbian? Marginal? All of these? None of them?" I formulate that mental question more often now that we've become friends on social media. That was what put me back in touch with many of the Indigenous people I had known before I left the Nation in order to get some distance, to do my best to figure out for myself where I belonged after living there all my life. I wasn't entirely successful, but I moved back anyway, to one edge of Dinétah.

Social media reawakened in me the knowledge that I still often didn't know where I fit. The awareness that I live in a fissure between cultures began with my public profile, which said:

Lives in: Gamerco, New Mexico
From: Teec Nos Pos, Arizona

Gamerco lies next to the border town of Gallup, and Teec Nos Pos lies deep in the Nation. Lily, someone I'd known at UNM and worked with closely in Diné bilingual education, saw my profile and wrote to me:

I see you're from Teec Nos Pos. I wonder if we might be related. My dad was from TNP.

She added her clan names, the Diné way of checking relatedness.

My name had changed since we last saw each other, or she would've known straightaway who I was. I wrote back telling her my former name. Then:

We ARE related but probably only as members of the human family.

Lily and I friended each other, and after that, I could count thirty-one Indigenous friends on social media, several more with strong ties to Indigenous communities, plus groups and pages that are mainly Native and keep me in touch with events and issues in the Indigenous world.

Most of the time, I enjoy a sense of camaraderie, and then sometimes I'm brought up short by the memes and statuses my friends post. When I see these, I ask myself, "How do you see me? Who am I in relationship to you?" And also, "Who are you? Maybe you are someone different from who I thought you were."

The meme's background is Disney-pink. Visually, it's a frame from the 1995 animation, *Pocahontas*. In the scene the beautiful young Indigenous woman lays her head on the shoulder of the stalwart, blond man. Their eyes are closed, but slightly wrinkled foreheads suggest trouble may lie ahead. The superimposed text reads, "I'm sorry but Masani[sic] says Bilagannas [sic] are *yee yah* [sic]."

What caught my attention when I first saw this meme on Facebook were not the spelling errors, which are common among many Diné who write in Diné bizaad. They write more or less phonetically rather than using standard written Diné bizaad. This is a phenomenon of the fact that literacy in Diné bizaad has been taught in relatively few schools, one facet of colonization. The existence of a standard written language is itself evidence of colonization. It is an instance of borrowing and adapting what is useful from the colonizers. The fact that I, a Bilagáana woman, notice the misspellings at all says something about how I fall into an odd crack between two languages and cultures. The great thing is that people are writing in Diné bizaad on social media, even when the writing is idiosyncratic. It's good because Diné bizaad is an endangered language, and every time and every way it is used provides it with more of a chance of surviving and flourishing.

What struck me hard about the words and image were the sentiment and the woman who had posted it. The text translates, "I'm sorry, but Grandma says White people are scary," and the implied message is, "Don't fall in love with a White person."

Tyna, a Diné colleague and friend, had displayed the representation. Not too long before it went up, she had messaged me asking for my help as a former school counselor in setting up a college scholarship fund for urban Indigenous youth in her community far from the Navajo Nation. I was happy to offer suggestions and delighted that she had thought of me as a resource. She posted a public thank you later.

A few weeks earlier, Tyna posted that she was craving blue cornmeal for ta'niil, the mush we like to make for breakfast. She couldn't find any in that far-off city, but I eat it often, and I know what it's like to be transplanted away from important food items. I mailed Tyna a few pounds of the gray-blue meal; again, she thanked me publicly on social media.

I am Bilagáana; there is no doubt about the color of my skin. I'm pretty sure that Tyna doesn't find me scary. But maybe a grandma would warn a Native man or woman against falling in love with me. My first reaction is, "Do you see me as scary?" My second thought is, "You're expressing your pain and anger. You are so right to do that. I understand." Third, I come back to, "How do you see me?"

There are many more layers to this meme. There is the heart-wrenching real-life story of what happened to Pocahontas. There is the Disney-fication of her story. There is the fact that intermarriage with

Whites is dangerous to the continued physical existence of Indigenous people whose survival is at stake. There is the acknowledgement that interracial relationships are subject to the burdens of a racist society. There is dark humor that may seem light to someone else, someone who doesn't carry the same baggage I do.

It is human to have feelings of antipathy toward groups and representatives of groups but love and warmth for individuals. That was how I reconciled Tyna's post with how she and I connect with each other. Nevertheless, I felt pain. I felt her pain and mine.

Robert is a Diné man, who is a master weaver, a visionary activist, and a networker who has taught Diné life-ways across ethnic and national boundaries. He is my friend on social media and in real life. We break bread together. We share common life stories. He is one of the most genuinely open, giving people I know.

One morning, Robert's status read, "My heroes have always killed cowboys," a play on "My Heroes Have Always Been Cowboys," the song popularized by Willie Nelson. It seemed so out-of-character for Robert. "This isn't you," I thought. But it probably is. Part of him—the hurt and angry part.

Several months after Robert posted that status, my friend Charlie, also Diné, posted a sepia-tone photo captioned "A Native American cowboy, ca. 1890." The man is tall and slim, has one pointy boot poised on a hay bale, a hand resting on his rifle, and is decked out in dressy cowboy clothes. Where does he fit? He is Third—both/and; he is not either/or.

I get a kick out of the inside humor on Facebook that many non-Natives might not see as funny. There are lots of fry bread jokes. There are jokes about Bluebird flour, the favored brand for making fry bread. A cartoon about smoke signals throws in an iPhone. Images of powwows and rodeos abound.

But sometimes the humor is self-deprecating. I get the jokes that make gentle fun of Indigenous stereotypes. I chuckle in recognition, but I don't feel I can "like" these memes because it might seem as though I were laughing *at*, not *with*.

As we approach the two autumn holidays of Columbus Day and Thanksgiving, posts exude both humor and underlying resentment. My favorite Columbus Day cartoon shows a man in a plumed hat with puffy breeches and tights trying to register at a hotel. The Indigenous clerk says, "I'm sorry, Mr. Columbus, but your Discover Card has been declined."

A common theme for Thanksgiving sketches shows Pilgrims rowing ashore. Natives watching them arrive make comments about turning away illegal immigrants. One stark cartoon shows a caricature of a Pilgrim and a single word, *Invaders*.

I've applauded when communities and states across the nation have renamed Columbus Day—— now Indigenous Peoples' Day. On the other hand, the dark humor telling White invaders to go home (and many other things) caused me at one point to write a letter to the nearest Dutch consulate and ask if I might be allowed to repatriate to the Netherlands based on my Dutch ancestry. I received an unequivocal no.

Being third means often not knowing just where to stand. A White woman once told me that I was difficult to get to know, that I seemed reticent. I realized, after she said it, that, in a new setting, I do sit back and watch, probably for a longer time than most. I'm observing, checking out the lay of the land. I'm finding out where I might fit in, whether it's safe to be known.

Sometimes my uncertainty is about when and how to use language. I'm not always sure a Diné person will welcome my speaking Diné bizaad. They might think I'm devaluing their competence in English. If they're much younger than I am, they may not know Diné bizaad at all, or they may know only a smattering and be uncomfortable, in case I might show them up. I try to feel my way around. I worked for two years with a Diné woman who is young enough to be my granddaughter. We would use a Diné word or two with each other now and then, but in all that time, I never did figure out how fluent she was, and she doesn't know the extent of my fluency, either.

Recently, I took a friend to Canyon de Chelly, a national monument within Dinétah. We stayed in the lodge at the mouth of the canyon, and the Diné clerk asked me at checkout, "Where are you headed today?"

"To T'iis Názbas." I gave it the Diné pronunciation.

"Hey!" She laughed. "You say it like a real rez girl. I can't even do that. I say it like a White girl." She seemed completely comfortable with the acknowledgement.

"I grew up there," I said, pleased.

The older woman who had checked us in, the afternoon before, was also behind the desk. She hadn't been especially friendly then, and now she scowled and said nothing. I didn't know if I'd insulted her English-speaking competence or if her countenance even had anything to do with me.

The variety of English I used regularly growing up was the creole called *Dummitawry English* by some linguists. My intonation still slips into Dummitawry English very slightly when I'm with Diné friends, or when I cross the border into the

Crevice 164

Nation. I catch myself after the fact. But I almost never use the phrases that were common to me as a young child. The singsong, "Ayyy," is a negation, kind of like, "Just kidding." "Is it?" can be asked, instead of, "Really?" As in: "I saw so-and-so at the Thriftway." "Is it?"

These expressions would feel to me like an inside joke, taking a friend and me back to our younger days. But, if I use them, it might be heard as a put-down or some form of appropriation. Occasionally I've risked it, and even with close friends, I've been unsure how to read the response, so I've stopped.

Recently, a White friend from Canada said to me, "People who have existed on multiple points of marginality have a different perspective. They have a richness to offer." My points of marginality consisted of life in a strong Dutch immigrant culture transplanted to the Navajo Nation; being a White child maturing within the Nation; being lesbian mostly beneath the surface while I was growing up; and all of this embedded in a highly conservative evangelical missionary culture.

I once told Ilene, a colleague in Diné education, a woman I'd known since we were children, that I thought I needed to remove myself because Navajo education should be run by Navajo educators. She said something similar to what my Canadian friend had said, "You have something unique to offer. You know our culture from inside and outside. You have a different perspective. We need different perspectives."

At the time, I couldn't let in what Ilene was saying, and although I thought I was leaving Diné education for altruistic reasons, I know now that I also left for myself. I needed distance to sort out an

Crevice 165

identity that was tangled up in the marginal cultures in which I'd grown up.

After I reconnected with Lily on social media, I shared with her some of the reasons that I had quit working in Diné education.

"Now I understand," she said. "Lots of times I said to Ellabee, 'I wish she would collaborate with us.'"

I was surprised all over again that what I had to offer had been valued more than I realized, that perhaps I didn't have to leave for that ostensibly noble reason. I felt that now I could give back, which was why I'd gone to that brainstorming session on language revitalization. I had a line on some seed money, and I said I would write a grant for it, but ultimately my offer came to nothing. Lily was part of the group, and I knew that she valued my participation, but when it came down to moving forward, there was a disconnect. At the time, I wondered if it had something to do with me, and only sometime later did I learn that it didn't.

Around that time, when Lily's students honored her as an elder, she included me in an email she sent to a small group—family members, her closest Diné friend from university, and me. She said she wanted to share the news with family and her closest friends. Again, I felt a wave of surprise. And also gratitude that Lily thinks of me in this way.

In Dinétah, I had negotiated a rich variety of communication forms. I'd spoken Dummitawry English with my friends. I'd absorbed the sounds of Diné bizaad and learned words and phrases, so I could often understand the gist of conversations and hold rudimentary exchanges on certain topics. I had learned to piece together meaning from fractured English. I learned to show respect as a child by swallowing an involuntary giggle when my Sunday school teacher referred to the holy man, Simeon, as Cinnamon. I had the unparalleled, highly valuable experience of being in the minority while belonging to the dominant group in the US. I could see when people were blissfully unaware that they were failing to communicate.

I put my inheritance to use outside Dinétah after I left. I worked with youth and parents in a Cambodian refugee agency in Oakland, California, where children served as their parents' interpreters during the day and ran with gangs at night. I started a community-based school in a church basement in conjunction with the public schools, and one of the Khmer boys who loved to talk about the Bloods and Crips said one day in a shift of allegiance, "We're Anna's Bloods." Later, I taught English as a Second Language to migrant workers' children on the Central Coast of California.

When I moved back to one of the edges of the Navajo Nation, Diné middle school students poured into my office on breaks between classes. They loved to test my knowledge of Diné bizaad and to teach me new vocabulary. For them and for me, my office became a little piece of home. When the fourth and fifth graders in Cuba suffered from racial antagonism among Hispanics, Anglos, and Diné, I held daylong sessions with them, designed to help them see that they were more alike than different and at the same time to help them appreciate each other's uniqueness.

All this I got from Being Third in Dinétah. And so much more.

The form asked for the usual—name, address, age. No thought required. Then the less usual—checkboxes for sexual orientation and what pronoun I preferred to go by. Easy. Then the last set of boxes: African

American, Hispanic, Asian, Caucasian, Pacific Islander, Native American, Other. I held my pen in the air over these options. What am I really? To look at my skin, I'm Caucasian, no doubt about it. Regardless of all those years spent in Dinétah, regardless of the Diné name Ella Descheenee gave me, regardless of the fact that I speak some Diné bizaad, regardless of my ability to read and write Navajo, I am definitely not Indigenous. So why hesitate? Why not do what I've always done? Check *Caucasian* without a second thought and be done with it?

I didn't. I lingered. And then I checked *Other*. For the first time ever. I had never considered this option before. I didn't plan it. But the thoughts I entertained in that pregnant pause went something like this: "My skin is white. All my life I have been heir to the privileges that come with being White. But, like everyone, I'm more than my skin color. I'm not Diné, but I share some traits, experience and knowledge with Diné that most Whites don't. The people who made up that checklist were probably thinking about ethnicity as it relates mostly to skin color, to genetics.

Many people exist on multiple points of marginality, living in the crevices between here and there. Many of us could check *Other* on a form. Being Other is Being Third. It challenges the binaries with which we know both comfort and discomfort. The fact of the existence of the Third cries out for a new paradigm for talking about, for living with, race and culture and intercultural contact. It also means that we are on our way to it, to a new model for living together.

The Obligation

"Do not be daunted by the enormity
of the world's grief. Do justly now.
Love mercy now. Walk humbly now.
You are not obligated to complete the work,
but neither are you free to abandon it."
~*The Talmud*

When we were children, our mother sometimes cooked up a pot of split pea soup for lunch. She flavored it with onions and ham hocks. The ham hocks not only tasted good with their pink saltiness, the sweetness of the fat, and the chewy, dimpled skin. They were packed with tiny squareish bones, which we cleaned with devotion until they shone slippery blue-white. It surprises me now, but our mother let us play with them, stacking them and lining them up on the table like houses along a street. In an unspoken understanding of the symbolism, we called the assemblage *Jerome*, the name of a ghost town we had visited in Arizona.

Near the end of high school, in the mid-nineteen sixties, I would think of those rows of bones as a diorama of Rehoboth Mission, the hub of our church's many smaller missions in the Navajo Nation. It was the place where I spent most of my school years, sometimes as a boarding student, sometimes as a day student, always as the child of White missionaries. I imagined a single knucklebone representing each house on the mission compound, a stack of bones as the institutional buildings—the hospital, the schools, the church. I had by then grown deeply critical of things I witnessed there, and I mentally connected the rows of knucklebones to Jesus' words: "Woe to you, teachers of the law ..., you hypocrites! You are like whitewashed tombs, which look beautiful on the outside but on the inside are full of the bones of the dead and everything unclean." That's how I felt about Rehoboth by the end of my schooling. The intensity of those feelings only grew as I moved into adulthood.

More than fifty years after I graduated, I have lived oceans away from the mission, and yet the mission is always with me. It continues to frequent my night dreams. In them, I usually I find myself in the high school, always in the hallway. It is dark there, the walls lined with military green lockers. Sometimes I am missing essential clothing, sometimes trying to get to class, never making it. Other times I have no pencils, and that is of vital and frightening importance. Each time, the dream ends when at last I remember that I succeeded in graduating from high school long ago.

The majority of dream researchers and theorists agree that recurrent dreams call attention to unresolved problems in the life of the dreamer and that a powerful dream image may provide a context for an unsettling emotion or conflict. Whenever I return to the mission in real life, whether for a nephew's graduation party or a wedding or a funeral, I feel those unfinished conflicts in my stomach—the ones symbolized by that long, dark hallway. I relive memories of times long past. I think of my Diné friends and stories they have told and continue to tell about their years at the mission. I remember my own years there. The dream that returns to me over and over tells me that there is something I have left undone. Maybe it is something that I, more than half a century after supposedly having finished with Rehoboth, am still obligated to do.

So many questions arise out of the brokenness that I was a part of, the main one being "What is my responsibility regarding this tear in the fabric of the world?" Because I grew up in Dinétah, I was the recipient of a wealth of experiences uncommon to most Whites. I ask myself if I owe more than others because of this. "Have these experiences equipped me in a way that also obligates me?" And, "Just how do I extend myself in a way that is truly helpful and meaningful without appropriating a task that might not belong to me?" I have been afraid to reach out a hand of reconciliation—afraid of doing it wrong, afraid of having any overture rejected, especially by people I care for. Afraid I will be misunderstood.

Fania Davis Jordan is a civil rights attorney and executive director of Restorative Justice for Oakland Youth. She also happens to be the sister of Angela Davis. The murders of Michael Brown and Eric Garner and the subsequent decisions not to indict the police officers who killed them served as the immediate impetus for her July 2016 article in *Yes Magazine*, "This Country Needs a Truth and Reconciliation Process on Violence Against African Americans—Right Now." I know I am not alone in finding the thought of a national truth and reconciliation process overwhelming, although I believe it is absolutely needed. I can't help asking myself if my nighttime journeys to those darkened Rehoboth hallways continue to plague me because my share in the history of the mission constrains me in a particular way to be part of a reconciliation process within the Navajo Nation.

Rehoboth Mission got its start in 1903. My high school history teacher, a former missionary kid, Bilagáana like me, told us that the land for the mission was obtained through the Homestead Act. He said that two Dutch women, Miss Russbach and Miss

Hartog, staked the claim. I imagined stern, intrepid women in long black dresses urging a team of horses from the seat of their buckboard wagon, dust swirling around them, leaping down to pound wooden stakes into the red earth. Since then, I've heard less colorful stories about the mission's inception. I don't know which story is true, but I know the one I prefer, if the mission had to exist at all. What I do know is that the mission caused great losses and damage to many Diné and Zuni children and their families, and also to Bilagáana children like me.

I date the beginning of my awareness of the injustices among Whites and Indigenous people earlier than my time at Rehoboth. It goes back to 1952, the year that I turned four. It was shortly after my father received his assignment as a missionary in Shiprock, New Mexico. At that time Shiprock was a tiny village in the northern section of the Navajo Nation, an emblem of colonization, since nothing had existed there before the US Government established it as one of its administrative locations. Our church's mission board provided us with a large two-story house in Shiprock. It stood on a hill, and from our living room, a large picture window looked down across a road onto the activity surrounding Jack's Trading Post. Standing at the window was like watching a movie, although I had never seen a movie at the time, so I would not have drawn that comparison then.

Diné people drove up to Jack's from miles around in horse-drawn wagons to unload bags of wool and piñon nuts, carefully folded rugs, silver and turquoise jewelry wrapped in flour sacking. They walked into the trading post with these and came out with bags of Bluebird flour slung over shoulders, cans of Folgers coffee, loops of rope, enamel basins, bags of sugar. After loading these into their wagons, some stood against the trading post walls or in the shade of gnarled cottonwoods exchanging news while their horses nosed into feedbags.

Sometimes visitors came to us from God's great Midwest. My parents treated them with deference because they supported the mission with money and prayers. It was during one of these visits that I date my earliest awareness of racism. I was playing on the floor in the living room, and the visitors stood at the picture window, watching the scene below them. One of them said, "Just look at those Indians down there."

I said without hesitation and a knife in my voice, "They're not Indians. They're nice Navajos." I'm sure I knew that the Diné could be called *Indians*; I objected to the tone I heard. I didn't know the word *racism*, but I didn't need to know it. I knew what I heard, and I didn't have to think at all about how I felt. I recognized the sound of injustice. I knew it was up to me to correct it.

No doubt my parents were embarrassed and scolded me for disrespecting adults. I hope the Midwesterners were discomfited by a child's righteous indignation. I wasn't punished, but I would have felt hurt because my mother and father misunderstood my intent.

My first playmates on the hill, Rudy and Bobby Yellowhair, lived in a white canvas tent close by our imposing, gray and brown house. They lived there year-round with their mother, Iva. In Shiprock, temperatures before climate change ranged on average from fifteen degrees Fahrenheit in winter to ninety-four degrees in summer. Someone had tried to make the tent withstand the weather better by nailing discarded slabs of wood ammunition boxes around its walls. In winter the tent was heated by a woodstove whose smoke pipe snaked up through a hole in the tent roof.

When it snowed, I worried about my friends. "Aren't they cold?" I asked. Quite possibly my parents offered Iva mittens and sweaters and caps with

Crevice 173

earflaps from the mission barrel. But I knew that tent couldn't be as warm as our house with its lovely radiant wall heaters. I didn't know the word *privilege*, but I knew there was an imbalance. I knew something was wrong, and I felt helpless about it.

When our class moved up to fifth grade at the mission school, a boy who had already done fifth grade joined us. Even the second time around, that grade was a struggle for Tom. And all the grades after that until our senior year, which was when Tom finally blossomed. We all got to see then how smart he really was. That was the year in which he at last mastered English, and everything else fell into place. That was the year I truly understood what it meant to come to school speaking no English, punished for speaking the only language you had. I wondered how my classmates had functioned at all. Later, I understood that they had received no special instruction in the learning of a second language. This was not language teaching through a carefully sequenced immersion strategy; it was sink or swim at the level of native speakers of English.

When our teachers at the mission school assigned written work in high school, some of my friends asked me to edit theirs. I was glad to do it, but sometimes I worried that the teachers would think we were cheating. Later, I learned the word *paternalism*, and at that point, I wondered if being a helper had been paternalistic. I wanted things to be equal, and maybe they were. The friend who most often asked me to edit her work had been a playmate when we were kids. She was the one who gave me my first Navajo cake from a girl's kinaaldá, her puberty ceremony, sharing with me a bit of the culture in which I was learning to live. We had ridden bikes together around the sheep dip and had sleepovers in each other's homes. Maybe it's not possible to measure equality in a friendship because the exchanges are both different and the same.

Crevice 174

All these things I saw and heard and lived with, and more and more I knew that something was wrong. I didn't have the words *racism, privilege, paternalism*, but I knew the reality from deep within, and I knew something needed to change. I just didn't know what or how or if it was up to me to do anything. Still in high school, I had arguments with my father about some of these things for which I had no words. I thought, especially after seeing how Tom and some of my other friends transformed along the way, that education was the answer, an equalizer. Education and love. It all came down to love, I thought. I said this one Sunday afternoon, and my father said, "Ach! You talk too much about love!"

I shot back, "How can I talk too much about love when the Bible says that God is love?" I stalked off on the high heels of Sunday, no love for my father in that moment.

In a recent interview with Terry Gross, David Oyelowo, a British actor of Nigerian descent, said of African Americans, if "your history is rooted in slavery, that really, I think, messes with your sense of self...." The same case might be made for the emotional impact of conquest and colonization on Indigenous peoples—that the less tangible effects on a sense of self are passed on from historical times to the present.

Recent studies reported in *Development and Psychopathology* confirm Oyelowo's intuitive understanding. They show that trauma is carried from generation to generation on the double helix of DNA. So the soul-crushing trauma suffered by the ancestors of my Indigenous friends lives on in them. Some of my friends have told me stories about things that happened to grandparents and great grandparents—The Long Walk of 1864 and the return in 1868, lost land, lost language. The list goes on. What happened at Rehoboth in the early 20th century is experienced not only through stories passed down,

Crevice 175

but also by those events that mark the genes.

Indignities continue today. Indigenous students are routinely forbidden to adorn graduation caps with beadwork or feathers. Male students with long braids have been suspended pending haircuts. Only after years of protests, did the Washington Commanders drop their racist name, *Redskins*. A national news anchor announced the patent ridiculousness that Natives are illegal aliens. In some states, public school curricula teach that Indigenous people are gone from the surface of the Earth, that they are people of the past.

On the bright side, genetic research also suggests that resilience rides on the genes from the fathers and mothers to the children and grandchildren. Attend a powwow, and you will see ample evidence of vibrant, thriving Indigenous cultures. I have friends who are master weavers of traditional rugs and sashes as well as users of new fiber art techniques combined with ancient methods and themes. I know painters who bring together current and past subjects with bold new styles and methods. Former colleagues work with intense love and creativity to keep Diné bizaad alive in the minds and mouths of Diné youth.

Despite the resilience, I am overcome by the deep knowledge that something is wrong, and it is not about Natives. Nor is it about non-Natives, rightfully called by some Indigenous people, *illegal immigrants*. It is about relationship. It is about brokenness. It is about a once bright potential for living in harmony that has been smashed by genocide, both cultural and actual.

The year 2003 saw the 100th anniversary of the mission at Rehoboth. Missionaries among Indigenous people are infamous for working hand-in-glove with governments to "pacify" or "civilize" Indigenous people. After "The only good Indian is a dead Indian," came the phrase, "Kill the Indian, save the man." And that was where missionaries came into the picture. I knew that Rehoboth's centennial celebration would include recognition of the damage the missionaries had caused to Diné and Zuni people, as well as an apology.

In righteous anger about incalculable damage, passed on to generations of those 1903 and subsequent Rehoboth students, I refused to attend the celebration. I believed that the apology would constitute a sort of whitewash (pun intended), a theater piece enacted, so that the mission could go on doing what it had done before, only more humanely now and with a lightened conscience. Admittedly, the school had changed markedly for the better since my friends and I were students. Instead of punishing students for speaking their Mother Tongue, being part of the elimination of the language, the school now taught Diné bizaad classes, thus becoming part of the general language revitalization effort. The mission had built a communications center honoring the Navajo Code Talkers of World War II. But to me this seemed to be too little too late. A Diné friend and colleague of mine would not even go to the mission for her mother's funeral in pain-filled protest. I saw my refusal to attend the celebration as an act of solidarity with her and others. And when I say that the mission intended to go on doing what it had been doing, I mean that it would continue proselytizing for Christianity—something I object to strongly.

My seven brothers did attend the celebration, including the reconciliation service, though *reconciliation* is really a misnomer. *Conciliation* would be a more accurate word, since *reconciliation* implies that there was once harmony that needs only to be restored between Whites and Indigenes, when in fact such harmony never existed. During the ceremony, three speakers (Rehoboth's executive director, a Diné church leader, and the director of the denomination's mission board) offered public admissions of guilt accompanied by apologies. They called their formal words "A Message of Confession and Reconciliation." Then there was time for responses from former students and parents. I heard about it all from my brothers.

One of them told me about a Diné woman I'd known since fourth grade. Carol was a year ahead of me in school. My brother said, "She got up and started crying. She said, 'I didn't think this day would ever come.'"

I felt some shame. Maybe I had been wrong. Perhaps the apology was more sincere than I had imagined. Or maybe the degree of sincerity had mattered less than the fact that an attempt at conciliation had been made at all, the recognition that an apology was needed. I have often said in situations that are far less grave—for example, when a retail worker apologizes to me, "Sorry goes a long ways with me." Maybe it was like that.

It is only right that churches, perpetrators of some of the gravest transgressions upon people who were once truly sovereign in their own land, should be some of the first to attempt conciliation. These are good and necessary beginnings. But the need for conciliation extends far beyond apologies from religious groups. The most well-known and largest government-sponsored truth and reconciliation process occurred in South Africa following the end of Apartheid. The people who conducted and participated in the truth and reconciliation process often did feel overwhelmed. One way that they dealt with the enormity of the task was to set limits—limits as to who would testify in public hearings and what forms reparations might take. Often reparation was a token, or it was creatively applied to a group. The process was not without its flaws and critics, but as the late Desmond Tutu, the head of the commission, reiterated, it allowed South Africa to make a transition to majority rule without the bloodshed that has occurred in so many other places following similar changes.

Fania Davis Jordan, in her *Yes Magazine* article, cites a few government-sponsored truth and reconciliation processes that have occurred in North America. The first to happen in the US was the Greensboro Truth and Reconciliation Commission in North Carolina, held in 2004 and focusing on actions by the Ku Klux Klan in 1979. Maine has an ongoing truth commission initiated by the state's governor and Indigenous leaders to address the forced assimilation of Native children in the state's welfare system. The Truth and Reconciliation Commission of Canada, only recently completed, undertook a much larger effort regarding the abuses of First Nations people (as Indigenous people are called in Canada) in residential schools. Even though the Canadian commission addressed a nationwide injustice, it had a limited focus—that of boarding school wrongs. Other commissions named by Jordan also limited their scope, and that may be the best way to begin a process of conciliation. As Martin Luther King, Jr., said, "Unless we learn to live together as brothers [and sisters] we will die together as fools."

It was social media that put me back in touch with many of the Diné friends with whom I'd lost contact. It was also social media that made me intensely aware of the level of pain and anger most are still living with. In addition, I see the strength, the ability to bounce back (or forward), the commitment to a healthful lifeway, the willingness to engage with joy and humor.

It was also social media that confronted me daily with the ongoing insults and long-lived wounds that my friends experienced. Every single time I read of them, I think, "Something has to change. We can't just go on like this, in this discord, this rupture between Indigenous people and the rest of us—

discord that most of the rest of us aren't even aware exists. That's got to be the first step—awareness."

The powerful sense that something must change motivated me to study truth and reconciliation processes that others—churches, governments, and individuals—have undertaken. In 2009, President Obama signed into law an official apology to Native people. In the words of the bill's sponsor, then Senator Sam Brownback (R-KS), the purpose of the Native American Apology Resolution was "to officially apologize for the past ill-conceived policies by the US Government toward the Native Peoples of this land and re-affirm our commitment toward healing our nation's wounds and working toward establishing better relationships rooted in reconciliation." It is always important to recognize beginnings, however small, in a healing process. However, such apologies do not go nearly far enough.

The healing model that seems most common is quite simple. It begins by giving those who have been wounded and also their descendants the opportunity to tell their stories, to tell what happened to them and their ancestors. Then the actual perpetrators or the representatives of the perpetrators acknowledge the offenses, take responsibility and offer their sorrow for what happened. Direct perpetrators must then change their behavior, and when institutions and governments are involved, reparations are necessary along with the changes. Reparations are most often thought of as monetary, but, as in South Africa, other types of restitution may be more meaningful and practical. For example, land that had been stolen was restored to its rightful owners. An instance of symbolic restitution involved the construction of memorials to victims of Apartheid violence.

Before I grasped this paradigm, I was always at a loss for words when my friends posted images and words in social media about horrible injustices and insults, past and present. I felt that anything I could say would be of little value, so I said nothing. Finally, finding a guide for conciliation showed me how I could respond, how I *must* respond at every opportunity, whether face-to-face or in writing.

My first chance came when a former colleague posted a photographic triptych on Facebook. The top two were sepia-tone boarding school photos. On the left were Native children with long hair wearing a blend of traditional and Anglo dress, looking angry. On the right they had shorn hair (boys) or hair pulled back in neat, tight buns (girls) and wore uniforms; they looked subdued, "pacified," as they used to say. Below these two was a color photo of Whites at a sporting event, decked out in feathered headdresses and face paint. The text read, "WERE THEY FORCED TO GIVE UP THEIR CULTURE SO YOU COULD DO THIS?"

I commented on my friend's post, "Thank you for posting this. I want you to know that I am deeply sorry for the damage that my people did and continue to do to your people. Deeply. We need conciliation."

My friend replied almost immediately, "Thank you, Anna." She added a heart emoticon, and I started to cry, really cry. Hard. Clearly, when there is a societal wound, we are all wounded and in need of healing.

My next opportunity to extend myself in a gesture of conciliation also took place online. A friend had posted the following quote by the late South African singer and civil rights activist, Miriam Makeba:

> The conqueror writes history; they came, they conquered, they write. You don't expect people who came to invade us to write the truth about us. They will always write negative things about us and they have to do that because they have to justify their invasion in all

countries.

I replied:

Thank you for posting this. I love
Miriam Makeba and her music, too.
More important here and now, thank
you for posting her words about
colonists and revisionist history to
justify the invasion and occupation. I
am deeply sorry for the pain and
damage my people caused and continue
to cause to your people. I hope for and
want to work toward conciliation.

I had been more hesitant when I wrote this
comment, less sure of the response I might get
because I have sensed more anger from Jennie, whom
I'd known in our mission boarding school days, than
from my former colleague. Sometimes, I had felt that
the anger might be directed at me, although it is often
hard to know for sure about emotions when the
communication is online rather than in person.

A few hours after I posted my response, my
friend "liked" my reply. Several hours later she wrote,
"Anna, thank you for being an ally."

I happen to be a member of a sexual minority,
and I know from a deep place how essential it is to
have allies in my life and in the lives of my people.
Once again, I was moved to tears. Jennie's response
was confirmation that I could begin where I was and
take advantage of every chance I had. It *has* to start
somewhere. I was saying, "I hear your pain. I want to
respond. I want to be part of a healing process. I don't
know how it will look, but I want to do it." I know that
each time I will be improvising, relying upon the
experience of those who entered this process before
me. Every time I responded to a friend's pain at
having been injured by my people, I learned

something new about the process. Jennie's two-step response, several hours apart taught me that it can take time for someone to absorb and respond to a reconciling effort.

A few weeks later Alice Whitegoat, a close friend, and I went for a walk in a Russian olive and cottonwood forest. Scattered among the trees lay small meadows, thick with foxtails and Queen Anne's lace. At one point we sat on a bench beside the path, and in the course of our conversation I asked her about her parents' decision not to speak Diné bizaad with her when she was growing up. I wasn't surprised to learn that a doctor at Rehoboth had given them advice that became the deciding factor.

We started walking again, and I took a deep breath after a short internal debate. "Alice, I've never said this to you before, but I am deeply sorry for the damage that my people have caused your people." We were walking side-by-side, but we paused and faced each other, and my mouth and voice started trembling. I felt tears coming. I didn't want that, didn't want to make Alice uncomfortable in any way, and I knew that my visible emotion could do that.

Alice seemed taken aback and made excuses for me. "It's not your responsibility. You were just a child." I think she meant that, as a child, I had had no more power in my situation than any of my Diné friends had had in theirs.

I knew there was an answer regarding my responsibility, but I couldn't think of how to say it, except for the Bible verse about the sins of the fathers being visited upon the children for generations to come. I didn't want to use that, in part because of our mutual mission school background, so I kept silent, and the moment passed.

Of course, what I needed to say came to me after we had left the forest and parted ways. It was this: "We're all in this together. Whether it's something we've inherited from way back, whether we are dealing it out or receiving it now. We're all in it. We're all affected by it. So we're all responsible for doing the healing work. All of us." We are not only all responsible; we are all in need of it. Desmond and his daughter Mpho Tutu pointed out in *The Book of Forgiving*,

> To walk the path of forgiveness is to recognize that your crimes harm you as they harm me. To walk the path of forgiveness is to recognize that my dignity is bound up in your dignity, and every wrongdoing hurts us all.

Talking with Alice in person offered what may have been the most important learning experience in personal conciliation I'd had by then. From it, I drew the conclusion that a face-to-face engagement probably requires some preparation. I could have seen this from Jennie's online response, which gave her all the time she needed, and from the fact that her response came in stages. I think when I am physically with someone, we must have an agreement that we are mutually entering a process with the goal of making things better. An agreement implies a more formal process, not something I might say off the cuff, as I did with Alice. At the very least, we need to be seated, making direct contact. It didn't help Alice that I got visibly and audibly emotional in that context, but if we had first agreed to talk about it, it might have been okay. As it was, I got the feeling that my attempt was just a source of embarrassment for her.

Another factor could be Alice's age and the mellowing that has taken place in her and that I've witnessed over the years. I think she has come to terms with many personal injuries, that she has in many ways moved beyond them, taking her own route to get there.

I have attempted the beginnings of personal conciliation a few more times. One of those attempts gave me even more information, although I'm not sure how to use it yet. I followed the same steps of acknowledging the damage, apologizing, and making a commitment to conciliation after a friend posted a disturbing meme about Hitler having admired and been influenced by the mass extermination of Indigenous people in the US. My friend did not reply to my comment. But two days later he thanked me publicly on social media for a gift that had been given several years earlier. I felt as though this was an indirect reply, and it has caused me to question the advisability of attempting online resolution to these gaping wounds. Improvisation most often involves trial and error.

The next question I ask myself is, "Where do I go from here, from these small, individual attempts?" As I told Jennie, I want to work for conciliation. I am convinced that individual efforts are needed, but they are not enough. On the other hand, the thought of trying to have an effect on the bigger picture is daunting. I keep reminding myself that others are already doing this work and that I don't have to do it alone. I've asked myself if I might join an existing group or find others who would want to engage in the work with me. I have also wondered if writing about conciliation—to make others aware of the need— might fulfill my obligation. It seems too little.

In addition to the question about responsibility, I have felt compelled to ask if I have a right to assert the need for conciliation. Should the impetus be coming from Indigenous people, not from me? Black filmmaker, Ava DuVernay wrote, "I'm interested in having people of color at the center of their own lives. We don't need to be saved by anyone. We do not need to have anyone sweeping in on a white horse or someone saving the day or assisting us in our own narrative."

"No," I reply mentally. "That is certainly not what is needed. Conciliation has to be an act of mutuality, of complementarity—healing for people on all sides. Otherwise, it will fail." I hasten to add that I only saw that short snippet from DuVernay, and I may well be applying it outside her intended context, but her words fueled my thoughts about what might be an appropriate role for me in a conciliation process.

I brought up the idea of a Truth and Conciliation Commission with Alice Whitegoat. "Do you think the motivation for a commission needs to come from Indigenous people? Do I have a right to work to make it happen?"

Without pausing, she said, "You have a right because you're a human being."

Right. Responsibility. Perhaps even joy. Kate Bornstein in *Gender Outlaw* writes, "Your life's work begins where your great joy meets the world's great hunger." Maybe this is what engaging in truth and conciliation work will be for me. Great joy. Perhaps it is not an obligation; perhaps it will be an oblation offered in joy.

In August of 2014, I attended the First Annual Indigenous Fine Art Market in Santa Fe. The day was chilly, gray and rainy, but spirits were high. The art, from all over the US and Canada, was powerful and haunting in its blend of the traditional with the avant-garde. Entertainment reflected that blend—break dancing, traditional hoop dances, time-honored musical groups and contemporary ones that mixed it up with both humor and gravitas.

Certain paintings sliced deep, bringing tears and sometimes laughter. I enjoyed conversations with artists about their work. I met with friends, shared food and coffee, sauntered with them among the booths. What struck me most powerfully, what I kept coming back to, was how this market, this festival of art and engagement, could serve as a model for a new way of being with one another. Every imaginable color of human was present—red, brown, beige, mahogany, gold, coffee, pink, butterscotch, blue-black, cream, rose, copper—strolling, laughing, talking. I never once saw a moment of conflict while I sat on a low stone wall with my friends and watched humanity stream by—babies, crones bent with age, youth with dreadlocks, young men wearing the traditional Diné hair bun, the bitsii'yeel. Clothing represented Africa, the Middle East, Indigenous America, and included dramatic couture that combined ancient themes with contemporary invention. I saw people from every continent on Earth, every ethnic strand and mix, enjoying, appreciating, learning from one another. Joying in each other's differences and commonality.

I thought, "This is how it could be. This is how we humans—the only race there is—how we need to be." That day gave me a vision filled with sounds and stunning images—a vision for a new way of being with one another in the US, across colors, shapes, sizes, ideals. But it was only a dream, a dream I would even have to call *sentimental*, if I don't find some way to be part of making it surpass meager happy thoughts of sisterhood and brotherhood.

A Reckoning

"A Third Culture Kid (TCK) is a person
who has spent a significant part of his or her
developmental years outside the parents' culture.
The TCK frequently builds relationships to all
of the cultures, while not having full ownership
in any. ... This lack of full ownership is what gives
that sense of simultaneously belonging
'everywhere and nowhere.'"
~ David C. Pollock and Ruth E. Van Reken,
Third Culture Kids

"Transformation is not accomplished
by tentative wading at the edge."
Robin Wall Kimmerer, *Braiding Sweetgrass*

Lily Roanhorse and I sat on the patio of the Farmington, New Mexico Holiday Inn with cold drinks after a day of training teachers in the use of our Navajo Bilingual Bicultural Curriculum Kit. Something she said prompted me to say, "A lot of the time I hide what I know about Diné culture when I'm with Diné people who don't know me."

Without missing a beat, Lily said, "You have an identity crisis, just like us."

"Us" in Lily's statement referred to college educated Diné, who were few in number in the early 1970s. Lily was right about one thing: I had an identity crisis. On the other hand, as a Bilagáana woman, I wasn't "just like us." I benefited all the time from privilege that accrued and continues to accrue to me, due to the color of my skin, and I knew it. I was grateful that Lily had seen me for who I was—an In Between—confused about my identity, about where and with whom I belonged, but I knew her gift went beyond the reality of our situations.

The word "identity" came into use in the English language around 1600 and comes from the Latin "idem," meaning "same" or "sameness." Thus, the attempt to establish our identity can be described as an attempt to discover what, who, or what group we are the same as. Or close to the same. Close enough to the same that we can "identify" with that group.

The first recorded use of the phrase "identity crisis" took place in 1954. In the "normal" scheme of things, there presumably will not be a crisis. Psychologist Erik Erikson proposed a theory of psychosocial development that became influential in White Western psychology. In his schema, formation of identity is the task of the pre-teen and teen years.

We've realized since his early work that these stages aren't as rigid as suggested by Erikson, even under "normal" circumstances. In the case of Third Culture Kids (TCKs), the development of identity can be a lifelong process. I am a TCK, or at this point, an ATCK (Adult Third Culture Kid). My parents were Dutch-American, evangelical Protestant missionaries in the Navajo Nation. They were still strongly connected through their denomination with a Dutch immigrant community, able to speak Dutch, despite being second- and third-generation American born. Theirs was my home culture, and, eventually, my school culture in the government and mission schools I attended in Dinétah.

During my developmental years in the 1950s and 60s, the Navajo Nation was postcolonial, and where we lived, especially initially, life was still mostly traditional—subsistence sheep-herding, farming, and artisanal economy, where people followed many of their traditional cultural practices. This was the larger context of my early life.

In my case, Erikson had been right in a sense— I did start his prescribed task of identity formation in my teen years, which he identifies as ages 12-18. However, it took until I was sixteen for me to fully internalize, in any appreciable sense, that I am White. I might never have pinpointed an actual event, had a my friend Janet, who is also White, not asked me once, far into adulthood, "Since race is a social construct, when did you first know you were White?"

Finding the answer took a good deal of pondering. Eventually, I knew the realization took place on a Sunday evening in a church service, where I was not listening to the sermon. I was worrying, preoccupied with the problem that had kept me awake nights during my entire senior year—how I was going to afford college. I knew my parents couldn't help me. A week earlier, the principal had shown up to one of our classes to tell the Diné students about the Navajo Tribal scholarship program, which would give them a full ride to any college they were accepted to.

In *Oxford Languages*, one definition of "acculturation" is "assimilation to a different culture, typically the dominant one." In my case, which sometimes feels like looking at myself in a funhouse mirror, often without the fun, I assimilated in certain ways to the nondominant culture that surrounded me. And yet my home culture spoke Whiteness and thus privilege. It is an ironic artifact of that privilege that it took my being denied something I wanted and felt I needed—a way to afford college—for me to fully absorb the social construct of my Whiteness. It may have been the first time I *felt* White. Or, maybe more accurately, I felt who I was not, as Robin DiAngelo in

White Fragility points out, "We come to understand who we are by understanding who we are not."

When I heard about the scholarship, I felt as though I were being cheated out of something my peers were receiving, and why shouldn't I get what they were getting? I had gone to the same schools, lived in the same places. Didn't that mean something? I also felt guilty for feeling cheated because I knew society had given me many advantages, to say nothing of the prejudices and abuses my peers were subjected to at the mission school and in the world at large—— prejudice and abuse I escaped, to my shame, whenever I witnessed it. That was when I absorbed who I am not and thus who I am, when it comes to race. I know race is itself an artificial construct. Yet it is a construct that matters greatly in our present society and in our history in the US.

The year prior to the one I mark as when I knew I was White, I had been the first White student to integrate the dorms at the mission school I was attending. The Diné students and I were assigned three-month work-detail rotations, and my first one was in the dining hall. There, two Diné girls and I waited on family-style tables at breakfast. The first morning, we showed up in the kitchen to begin filling serving bowls with oatmeal. One of the assistant cooks, a desiccated old White woman, rushed over to me and hugged me. She'd never hugged me before, and she didn't hug the other two girls. I was embarrassed, ashamed even, and wanted to say something to the others, but what could I say? I swallowed the feeling of wanting to gag, and after that I kept my distance from this woman.

That was a small enough incident, but it was one of the many times I would know I had gotten special treatment because I was White. So maybe, in some way, I realized my Whiteness earlier than I think. I don't know what my Diné peers thought, but they never commented on it or treated me differently because of it.

What came out of those experiences for me was a growing sense of unworthiness—unworthy to even be a guest in Dinétah, undeserving to have been included in everyday Diné culture, unworthy because I represented the Whiteness that was my first heritage—a heritage of genocide both actual and cultural.

That feeling of unworthiness has persisted to this day, but it culminated in deep grief one night when I was attending summer school, getting my master's degree at the University of New Mexico (UNM). It happened that I was subletting Lily and my friend Ellabee's apartment, and in their record collection I found Lakota musician Floyd Westerman's 1969 album *Custer Died for Your Sins*. In the dark of that summer night, I listened to the title cut again and again, weeping uncontrollably.

At UNM, I studied Diné bizaad formally for the first time and also linguistics and bilingual education, which seemed a natural continuation of things I had learned growing up. What followed was years of being a member of various teams working on Diné education projects or teaching in largely Diné classrooms. Most often I was one of few or the only White person involved, and that felt like a privilege and also normal.

And then I left Diné education, believing leadership there should come from Diné educators themselves. That was only part of the reason, but it took time for me to understand that it was also because I still hadn't really figured out who I was. I couldn't begin to find out while I remained embedded in Dinétah.

While I was away, I rarely connected with my Diné friends. I was more often in touch with Ellabee than anyone else over the years. She had long been aware of my identity struggles. We'd known each other as kids attending the same mission school and over time had been university housemates and work colleagues. One summer evening, the issue of my identity came up. Ellabee tried to console me, saying that with my coloring, I could be seen as biracial— Diné and White. She suggested I sprinkle my speech with Diné slang, as one of our Bilagáana friends often did. While I was touched by her encouragement, I was also uncomfortable. I felt I'd be appropriating something that didn't belong to me, including imagining my ethnic makeup to be different from what it is. I'm sure that in today's climate, Ellabee would not offer those ideas, but I know they came from the heart and with more compassion than I could muster for myself.

With the advent of social media, I reconnected with Diné friends I'd lost touch with—like Lily and Alice Whitegoat, who had been my boss in a Native publishing house. The renewed friendships were satisfying, but I was still unable to let go of my identity struggles and move on. Reconnecting also happened in real life, and at times my grappling intensified then rather than fading.

Nearly every novel written in 2020 and in the years that have followed, addresses the impact of the pandemic, if it's set in present time. I've gotten somewhat inured, thinking, gratefully, that it hadn't affected me so much, which wasn't even close to the truth. I did not lose any family or close friends; however, late in 2020, I uprooted myself and moved from my Southwest home to a foreign country—rural, small-town Iowa, population approximately 600. No mesas, no canyons, and I virtually never saw a Black or Brown person. Before I moved, I had been alone in my bubble, sheltered in place, and I grew increasingly depressed. I had started noticing some cognitive losses, so I moved to this small town in order to have one other person I could freely engage with—my daughter who works in a museum here.

I didn't expect to ever work in Diné education again, and living in Iowa made that even less likely. By this time, I had retired as an educator and now focused on writing and translation. Then, one night in early 2021, I got a call from an unfamiliar number in Gallup, New Mexico. Because it was Gallup, one of the towns that borders Dinétah, I picked up. It was Ellabee, who didn't know I'd moved to this foreign land, so we spent some time catching up on each other's lives. Then she said, "I'm calling on behalf of the Diné Language Teachers Association (DLTA). We got a grant from the Kellogg Foundation to develop a home- and community-based Diné language revitalization project. We want to hire an evaluator to help us with data interpretation, and we're holding a group interview by conference call with several Native candidates. We'd like to include you. Are you available Wednesday evening at 7 p.m.?"

Because Diné bizaad has a larger pool of speakers than any other US Indigenous language, it has also had more staying power than many others. However, due especially to past damaging assimilationist US Government policies, including the prohibition of the use of the language in schools, widespread enforced boarding school attendance, relocation programs, increased numbers of paved roads, and the widespread availability of English language media, the use of Diné bizaad and the number of fluent speakers is now in rapid decline. In 1980, 93% of Diné spoke the language fluently. In 2017, only 57% were fluent. Based on an ever-increasing drop, it's projected that if things continue as they have been, only 10% of Diné people, mainly of the grandparent and great-grandparent generations, will be fluent in the language by 2030.

I agreed to participate in the interview, but as the day approached, I felt anxious. I didn't know the other candidates, and I would be the only White person involved. Even though I'd spent so many years being the only Bilagáana in countless settings, much of the time not even noticing it, this upcoming interview felt different. These younger Diné professionals didn't know me. They didn't know I'd grown up in Dinétah, gone to school there, taught and written bilingual curriculum and trained teachers there. They didn't know I read, wrote, understood and spoke some Diné bizaad. Of course, when I introduced myself, I could tell them some of these things, but that would feel a bit like saying, "Some of my best friends are...."

Call it a Freudian slip, but I missed the call, perhaps due to the time difference. I thought, "Okay. An opportunity missed. They probably wouldn't've hired me anyway, and why should they? They should hire someone Indigenous."

Ellabee called me later. "We still want to interview you."

I was surprised. It was a relief not to have to engage with the rest of the candidates, as the board would be talking just with me. After the interview, I remembered how much I loved working with language and thinking about language needs and changes with others. In the grip of my passion for the necessity to reverse the rapid loss of Diné bizaad, I sent a follow-up email to the board. It was filled with probing questions I thought might be useful to the team, regardless of who they hired. I also wanted to know more details about the project. Lily, who was then the board president, responded thoughtfully to my questions in a satisfying exchange.

More than a month elapsed following the interview, and I assumed that one of the other candidates had been chosen, which seemed right to me. Then I received another call. It was Ellabee again. "We want to hire you as our evaluator." I didn't ask why they chose me over the other candidates, but I wondered. Ellabee said one thing that may shed light on my unasked question: "I know how your mind works." I knew, too, that it was possible I wasn't the board's first choice.

When I joined the DLTA team, I asked them to pay me a dollar, making it symbolically clear that I was an employee. I might have said something about giving back, but I didn't say how keenly aware I was of the tremendous riches I'd received while growing up in Dinétah and as an adult working in a movement to redress some of the ills of colonialism.

One of the Kellogg Foundation's models for evaluators is participatory; thus, I became an integral part of the team. I offered ongoing feedback, instigated an examination of the project's direction early on, and I was part of a decision to apply a home-based language immersion approach that had been used by other Indigenous revitalization projects but not within the Navajo Nation, as far as we knew.

When I had suggested we take a step back to examine the course to which the team had first pivoted when the pandemic hit, Lily, who had co-founded the organization, resigned. It was the first time in my work as the only White on a Diné team that I didn't assume it was my fault that something so potentially devastating had happened. Lily made it clear that she was stepping back because of things going on in her personal life, and I fully trusted her.

The fact that I believed Lily represented an inner change. It gave me hope that working for DLTA might help shift how I saw myself within the fissure between worlds. I hoped I might have gained enough maturity to be finished with the identity issues that, per Erikson, should have been resolved decades earlier.

After Lily left the board, there were only three of us on the team—Ellabee, a Diné language teacher who was still in the classroom, and me. The pandemic had taught us about tools for collaborating remotely. We met once a week and worked hard researching our chosen approach, writing a handbook for participants, setting up a pilot project, holding a remotely held conference, and providing training sessions for our beta testers. We also joked and laughed. For those hours, I felt as if I were back home in Dinétah—my Home Not Home.

Dr. Bettina Love, a Black professor at Columbia, who teaches future educators and helps establish abolitionist teaching in schools, refers to people of color as "dark folx." She says that if White people are to be co-conspirators in abolitionist teaching, we must want "dark folx to thrive," and we must give "up power and positions in order to do so." When I read these words, I realized I've done this several times in my adult life. I did it in the day-to-day—waiting for others to speak in the publishing house, on the DLTA team and in schools. I did it by leaving Diné education behind for the leadership reason, even though underlying that was the need to discover my own identity. I knew I would do it again when it was time for me to leave the DLTA project.

Even before the teacher left the DLTA team because of her classroom duties, I'd been encouraging the skeletal board to recruit more members. After she left, it became even more critical. In the meantime, at every public, remote appearance we had, Ellabee asked for my input. I might agree to narrate a Power Point slide or two, but really, I wanted to stay in the background. That wasn't entirely to empower dark folx; it was also because I worried about how the Diné who made up most of our audience would see me. I imagined them asking, "What do they need her for?"

There were two reasons I might not qualify to be on the DLTA board. The two criteria for membership are being a Diné language teacher and being Diné, although the latter is not explicitly stated. Once when I said I didn't qualify because I wasn't a Diné language teacher, Ellabee contradicted me. "You are," she said. "You taught me how to read and write Diné bizaad."

"I didn't know you remembered that," I said. I was grateful that she did, and I enjoyed the recollection of us riding across Dinétah in my red-orange VW, named Łííʼ Łichííʼ (Red Horse), teaching her the phonics of Diné bizaad as we passed through pine forests and between red rock formations.

Not being Diné remained. I wasn't fluent in the language, either—another unstated obstacle.

For more than a year, our team consisted of just Ellabee and I, and I kept reminding her that our twosome wasn't sustainable. Finally, she began to recruit people she thought could serve the board well, and we held our first remote interviews. For the first time, during more than two years of our collaboration on the project, Ellabee introduced me as Bilagáana. Of course it's true, and it's fairly obvious on Zoom, but I was stung. Why now? During the interviews, I forced myself to speak a little Diné, and I could hear how strong my accent had become, due to a combination of stress and having been away from Dinétah for too long. In the aftermath, sitting in my darkened living room, I wanted desperately to disappear, to be erased. And yet I wanted to be seen.

Sometimes, no matter how right it is, giving up power and position in order for dark folx to thrive is painful. The distressing loss is much deeper and more intimate than a loss of power or position. It is the loss of connection, of involvement in something important, something essential, something deeply believed in. And there's no denying that, within me, I continue to believe letting go is the right thing to do.

About a year into the DLTA project, after spending more than five years trying to find my way into writing a memoir about how I'm related to the Diné world, I gave up. I decided to write about my identity struggles and how they fit into a larger picture, as autofiction. The big picture was about how we as humans negotiate intercultural contact, how we might heal that raggedness in our lives, in our world.

Crevice 198

And I worried that maybe it was grandiose of me to think I could even address the big picture. As humans, we seem to have failed so spectacularly; what made me better equipped than anyone else?

After more than a year of working on this novel, several things converged to make me realize I had been fictionalizing my life story for the wrong reasons. The realization was nothing short of an epiphany, and it brought me to a cold stop at page 274. The first event was the ongoing DLTA project and both the healing and the pain it brought to the fore.

Then there was a book club of two, formed by my friend Janet and me. We meet every week to read books about social justice and racism. We discuss books like *The Sum of Us* by Heather McGhee and *The Inconvenient Indian* by Thomas King. Thoroughly and deeply, we relate our learning to our life experiences. Some of my own reading paralleled what we read together, and the writings coalesced to make me realize, as I read *White Fragility* by Robin DiAngelo, how much I wanted to see myself, largely because of my experiences in Dinétah, as different from other Whites when it comes to Whiteness, White superiority, and systemic racism.

I recalled an incident from my teen years. It showed me that I'd wanted others to see me as different for a very long time. In Red Valley one summer, I was part of a mostly Diné youth group with a few White missionary kids sprinkled in. Mrs. Redhorse greeted me in Diné bizaad by name and handed me a bowl of mutton stew.

I greeted her as "shimá." My mother. Any Diné woman my mother's age ought to be greeted that way, but I'd also known her, the Diné missionary's wife, since I was four or five. I grabbed an industrial sized shaker and let it rain salt into my stew.

Mrs. Redhorse laughed and said, "You're just like us. You love salt."

Crevice 199

I hoped the Bilagáana kids heard her. That they knew I was different from them. Special. Later, it would be the Diné kids I hoped saw me as less White.

A third strand in the confluence that led me to abandon the novel was my work as a Danish-to-English literary translator. I had had uncomfortable experiences when I lived in Denmark where, as a White woman, I was sometimes included among "us" as opposed to "them"—people who came from dark roots.

Back in the States, I translated *With Sword and Pistol: Christian Madsen's Life and Experiences*—an autobiography of a Danish immigrant who had joined the US military in the late 1800s and later served as a lawman in what was then known as *Indian Territory*. Madsen, unlike many Whites of his time, actually knew Indigenous people as friends and showed them respect. Even though this information came in his own words, he had no reason, when he wrote the book in the early 20th century, to gild the lily. In fact, he might have had reason not to mention this. Nevertheless, his work involved military conflicts with Indigenous people and enforced their containment on reservations. I felt uneasy, in case my Diné friends learned I had translated this book. The words weren't mine, but I had given them voice in English. I did the work because I enjoy the challenges of translation, but I also gained financially from it. I realized I didn't want to be associated with it.

The final stream to join the confluence was the writing of the autofiction itself. The act of writing changed me, as our writing can. It caused me to realize I was writing my life as fiction, so I could feel comfortable justifying, explicating, how different I was from other Bilagáanas, how special I was.

The most recent book Janet and I had read at this writing was *We Want to Do More than Survive: Abolitionist Teaching and the Pursuit of Educational*

Freedom by Bettina Love. I can't begin to say what I as a White human and a retired White teacher learned from this book and from probing my life experiences in its context, but two things contributed tremendously to the transformation of how I see myself in relationship to the Diné world. Though I learned many things I believe Dr. Love would have wanted me to, the two most germane to the resolution of my struggles might not be what she was thinking about. Or, then again, maybe they are.

The first came early in the book, where Love described how her mother and grandmother insisted that she always live her life with dignity. I connected this with my pervasive sense of unworthiness in Diné settings. Low self-worth and self-dignity do not go together. Some of that sense certainly has come from guilt and pain by association with my settler heritage. But much of it also comes from the familial and church-based shaming that was embedded in my growing up years. Because of it, learning to walk with self-respect in whatever world I find myself in requires pretty constant awareness and commitment from me, and often I'm unsuccessful.

What came second, in the last chapter of Love's book were the words "Knowing who you are ... is healing." There is no denying that I am someone with a deep and pervasive experience of living between two markedly different, often conflicting, cultures. Books I'm most drawn to tell the stories of other In Betweens. Most often, the In Betweens are people of color—biracial people, children of immigrants who are caught between worlds, people like Lily who have in some way stepped outside their community's expectations. My professional life has most frequently been with people struggling to negotiate more than one culture. It's where I'm most comfortable, or as one of my brothers says, "comfortable with being uncomfortable."

I won't be surprised if such deep-seated feelings of unworthiness crop up again, but I've tasted freedom from that. That freedom makes any giving back, such as my work with DLTA, cleaner. Even before this transformation, as I worked on the project and others like it, being aware of my insecurities helped me not to act on them. The difference is that now I've known freedom from them. I've accepted that, yes, I do belong somewhere within the Navajo Nation—no longer near the center, where I once lived physically. But wherever I live on the Planet, I will never be far from the edges of Dinétah. I've accepted that Whiteness is and will always be a part of me, that it has shaped me, just as growing up and living in the Diné world has shaped me. I recognize that settler heritage is not my only heritage; I also inherited untold numbers of gifts living where I did. Like my Diné friends, I also belong there, but my belonging is different from theirs. I belong as a nearly lifelong guest. I can now be grateful that these friends have time and again affirmed my place, even when I couldn't accept their assertions. Moreover, and this feels incredibly significant, I am freed to simply be a friend to my friends, to enjoy the richness of our friendships in the ordinariness of the day-to-day.

Acknowledgements

Thank you to the people, both Diné and Bilagáana, who gave me the exceedingly rich life I experienced in Dinétah. The stories of what happened there have formed these essays. I am grateful for all of those encounters—the meaningful, the beautiful, the difficult. Thank you to the readers and editors of the journals, the anthology, and the newspaper that wanted to publish seven of the essays—*Clockhouse Review, Dove Tales Literary Journal, Fertile, Gallup Independent, Isthmus,* and *Solstice.* Thank you to the readers who have spread the stories to others and, to my astonishment and joy, the people who used them with their university classes. Lastly, thank you to you who read these essays, always in prior shapes and conditions, to help me make them the best I could: Louise Benally (Diné), J. D. Dolan, Stuart Dybek, Gloria Emerson (Diné), Monica Friedman, Jaimy Gordon, Joy Harjo (Muskogee-Creek), the late Sonja Horoshko, April Johnson, Jody Keisner, Janet Mason, Rose Fasthorse Nofchissey (Diné), Ann Przyzycki, Paolo Renigar, Catherine Robinson, Sarah Rodlund, Molly Jo Rose, Carl Ross, Ed Singer (Diné), and Art Winslow. Thank you to Tracy Roberts who selected *Crevice* as the winner of the Kenneth Johnston Nonfiction Book Award and for her kind words recognizing this work as valuable. Thank you to Ruth Heflin, my editor and book designer at Choeofpleirn Press, for her sensitivity and respect in making this a better book and for always considering my wishes in the process. Thank you to my brother Rick for his frequent generosity in offering the solitude and beauty of his Zuni Mountain cabin for personal writing retreats.

About the Author
Anna Redsand

Photo by Louise Benally

Anna Redsand shares many characteristics of other Adult Third Culture Kids (ATCKs), having spent most of her developmental years in a culture other than that of her parents. Perhaps the most notable of those traits is restlessness; she has moved seventy-one times, lived in three countries on as many continents, in all four hemispheres, and in eighteen US communities. She has also enjoyed living on the road. Life between postcolonial Diné (Navajo) and White cultures has deeply influenced her writing.

Anna's previous memoir, *To Drink from the Silver Cup*, explores the intersectionality of religion, spirituality, and sexuality in her life. Her first book, *Viktor Frankl: A Life Worth Living,* is a biography of the Holocaust survivor and author of *Man's Search for Meaning.* Her essays, poems and stories have been published in *Solstice, DoveTales, Isthmus, Clockhouse, Fireweed, Rockhurst Review, Mount Hope Magazine, Spaces, Friends Journal,* and *Gallup Journey.* They have also been anthologized in

Wet and *Fertile*. Her essay "Naturalization" was notable in *Best American Essays 2014*. Most recently she co-authored an article in the monograph, *Honoring Our Indigenous Languages and Cultures*. Diné readers of her work have said her voice is both important and essential.

Today, Anna works as a writer, a Danish-to-English translator, and an editor. She has worked as a linguist, educator, psychotherapist, hospice caregiver, operating room technician, housecleaner, and supermarket cashier. She enjoys travel, hiking, and engaging with other readers. She also makes fiber art and paper collages. She lives far from her Southwest home in the Danish Village of Elk Horn, Iowa, to be near her daughter and grandchildren but gets back to Navajo Country as often as possible. Anna identifies as a cisgender lesbian.

Previous Publications

"Fissures and Crenellations" was first published in *Solstice*.

"In and Out" was first published in *Isthmus*.

"Naturalization" was first published in *Clockhouse*.

"A Good Stranger" was first published in *Isthmus*.

"Tongues" was first published in *Fertile: An Anthology of Earth Poems and Prose from the High Desert and Mountains of the Four Corners Region*.

"Racial Injustice Benefited Me" was first published in *The Gallup Independent*.

"The Obligation" was first published in *DoveTales*.

Judge's Comments
2024 Contest Judge: Tracy Robert

In *Crevice,* Anna Redsand graces us with a memoir that is so much more than the genre implies. It is a meditation on family, on belonging in community, and on language, but it is also a paean to the Diné (Navajo) culture she grew up in and an apology for the practices of her Calvinist missionary parents who sought to quash the culture she loved.

The gorgeous prose of *Crevice*—somehow, miraculously, both vivid and spare—moves seamlessly from youthful recollections to present-day reflections. Diné friendships help Redsand see that there is "more than one pathway to the Infinite," contrary to the lockstep religious teachings of her parents. The mission school forbids use of the Navajo language, Diné bizaad, which she wishes to learn, and later in life the author realizes "when we take something from one group of people, everyone loses."

A beloved Diné family friend gives the author a childhood name that translates to *Girl Who Reaches After Things.* The book is an elegant and eloquent reaching, a bridge spanning the crevice between the Diné world Redsand wishes she could completely belong to and the hybrid world of "Home Not Home" she makes peace with accepting as hers.

Tracy Robert is the author of *Angora Panties: The Afterthoughts of Loss*, which won the Kenneth Johnston Nonfiction Book Contest in 2023. She also wrote the novel, *Flashcards and the Curse of Ambrosia*, published by New Rivers Press in 2016.

Choeofpleirn Press

Winner and finalists of the
Jonathan Holden Poetry Chapbook Contest 2024

Winner and finalist of the
Kenneth Johnston Nonfiction Book Contest 2023

Tracy Robert's mother in a photo used on a brochure and banner for LACMA's Gilbert Adrian exhibition. She was a beautiful, complicated, difficult woman, and it was hard to be her daughter. *Angora Panties: The Afterthoughts of Loss* is about Robert making peace with her mother's memory, among other things.

www.ingramcontent.com/pod-product-compliance
Lightning Source LLC
Chambersburg PA
CBHW061737120626
46550CB00005B/1819